MOONEY

MOONEY

The Life of the World's Master Carver

John P. Hayes

P.O. Box 350, Midvale, OH 44653

Cover by Grace Izold, Medina, Ohio

CONTENTS

Foreword vii
Introduction xi
The Missing Link 1
Frieda 17
Apprenticeship 26
The Steel Mill 37
The New York Central 48
Kinship 57
Golden Years of Carving 76
Nickel Museum 89
The War Years 100
April 7, 1947 111
Mooney's World 119
The Final Years 129
Book Notes

Foreword

One of the words we use to describe certain people is 'genius.' Almost always it makes us think of something like 'scientist,' or 'mathematician' or even, perhaps, of a name: Shakespeare, say. Then we remember that there are other kinds such as musical geniuses, sculptors, painters and so forth.

Genius is much more than talent or aptitude. If you look the word up, and I did, you'll find that it goes far back to the time of the early Romans and meant something like a personal "God." To be, or to have genius, one needed help beyond what man could give.

Mooney Warther was a genius. He had a personal "tutelary divinity" who guided his fingers. To people like me, who can't whittle a stick, Mooney was every bit as good as Michelangelo or Cellini. And, to judge by what we know of those gentlemen, Mooney was a nicer guy.

Mike Douglas knew I was a railroad buff and one day, back when his TV program originated in Cleveland, he invited Mooney to bring his Lincoln train to the studio—just as a surprise for me. Mike had no idea what labor was involved, how far Mooney had to travel, what it took to arrange the transport of this enormous work of art, etc. etc. It was just something he did for me, his friend. As they say, little did he know.

Little did he know! I took one look from ten feet away, slowly rose to my feet, walked over to the display and for what I think was the first time in my life, my jaw dropped. I mean, ladies and gentlemen, the real thing. My lower jaw detached itself from the upper. I regained control of it but, even though I waggled it and tried to get my voice box to work, no words came out.

The man was a genius.

It isn't true that I can't whittle a stick; I've been making models of trains a good part of my adult life. That's how I knew what the beauty was, the talent, the creative ability, the dexterity—all right, one more time, what the genius was that went into that train model. I should have said that compared with *Mooney Warther* I couldn't whittle a stick.

Later I was privileged to visit him at home and to discover what a delightful human being he was. He looked out at the world with a kind of cheerful innocence. Over the years of showing schoolchildren through his tiny museum he had developed a way of projecting his voice so that even when just the two of us sat together and were shooting the breeze his voice carried over the hills. It had a bounce to it, a vibrancy, and I always felt that at any second Mooney would shout "Hurrah!"

He probably knew less about money than anybody I ever met. He didn't know about it because he really didn't care. He didn't *need* money the way you and I do. There was nothing on earth he wanted to buy. As long as his museum stayed open, as long as buses full of kids arrived, he was delighted.

Speaking of which, the kids I mean, it's too bad that adults think that the kind of work Mr. Warther did was for children. Very few grownups, as far as I know, ever realized that what they were looking at was as magnificent as what is commonly called "fine art."

I think it goes something like this. An ordinary woman may not be a work of art but we agree that the Venus di Milo is. An ordinary locomotive may not be a work of art, but Mooney's impression of it certainly is.

A few years ago when I decided to move to Canada for personal reasons I sold all my furniture and all my chess sets. I had eighteen, including two of the rarest in the world. I sold everything but some clothes, a few snapshots, and my railroad chess set that Mooney made for me. I still have it, of course.

Like some other works of genius, nobody can afford it. Not while I'm around.

Henry Morgan

Introduction

There were days when I thought I might never finish this book about Mooney Warther. The loneliness of writing, the tediousness of editing, the anxiety about its being published and well received, often overcame me and my typewriter. What encouraged me, though, and what forced me to complete the manuscript, was my subject himself. On those days when I was discouraged I would think of Mooney Warther, particularly the Mooney Warther of 1923 who spent five lonely months on a train promoting the railroad. He wanted desperately to continue carving his Evolution of the Steam Engine, but he couldn't. Then later, just prior to the Depression, Mooney's wife fell seriously ill and his life's savings was depleted. He was frustrated again and again he was detained from completing his project. Eventually, of course, he finished it. I would think of Mooney Warther on those days and I could hear his voice booming, "Think that you can and do." How could I not? Inspired and eager, I would return to my typing table and continue writing.

Thus, this story of the life of the world's master carver, who I , like so many before me and with me, but few after me, had the pleasure of knowing and appreciating. The story, as I have recounted it, is not nearly so awesome as the events and contributions of the life itself. Yet, it is a story that enhances those events and contributions. It is a story that depicts the dedication, the perseverance, the agony and the joy of a man who lived according to his conscience and his whims. "I live each day the way I wish the world should be even after I am dead," Mooney Warther wrote in his diary. If Mooney were alive, he'd be disappointed. No matter. Mooney is gone. But he left the world his story.

This biography could not have been written, however, without the assistance of the following persons, to whom I am most grateful: Dr. Fred Bay, Lawrence Carmola, Leonard Contini, Kenny Espenschied, Mattie Finzer, Charlie Going, Ann (Scott) Harvey, Martha Hollinger, the Rev. Mr. Reinhard Krause, Vic Kuhn, Mrs. Mervin Lahmers, Chuck Mathias, Bruce Mears, Anna Meese, Johnny Meese, Mrs. Boots (Susan Wendling) Mizer, Tom Moore, Jr., Caroline J. Pardee, Hiner Richard, Walter Richard, Herm Rieker, Bill Shell, Dorothy (Eiler) Soulsby, Dale Warther, Don Warther, Fred Warther. I am also grateful to the late Don Frary.

I appreciate the assistance of Marilyn Lab, librarian, Dover Public Library; and John Grant, research assistant, Temple University. Also, the assistance of James E. Davis and Richard J. Farrell of the *Times-Reporter* who granted access to important photographs and newspaper clippings and to Joseph Conidi who supplied several rare photographs left to him by the late Charlie "Fat" Grunder.

Frieda Warther, who is now a spry eighty seven, contributed significantly to this work as did her sons David and Tom, and her daughter, Florence. They provided me with family documents and information that would not have otherwise been available. For that, I am grateful. Credit is also due David Warther, Jr., who is an expert on the life of his grandfather and who shared his wealth of material with me.

I am indebted to Professor Jacqueline Steck of Temple University for editing the original manuscript; to Professor Irene Sarbey of Kent State University for teaching me about writing; to Mary Folger, editor of *The Western Reserve Magazine,* for being there; to Robert D. Maloney, my uncle, for his encouragement; and to Louis A. Contini, my uncle, for his enthusiasm about this project.

Also, I thank my wife, Jo Ann, who's special, and our lovely daughter, Holly Lynne, who's delightful.

Finally, and perhaps most importantly, I thank my parents, Paul and Dolores Hayes. For it was they who had the foresight to raise a kid in Mooney Warther's back yard.

Philadelphia   JPH
June, 1977

FOR MY GRANDPARENTS

Rocco J. Contini
and
his late wife
Constance (Fazi) Contini

———

Anna (Erhart) Hayes
and
her late husband
Charles T. Hayes

Chapter One

The Missing Link

Mooney Warther must have told the story at least once for every day that he lived. People always wanted to know why he had started carving and no matter how many times he told the story he always repeated it with as much enthusiasm as the time before. It was as much a part of him as his wavy, white hair and his bellowing voice. Mooney Warther was a showman and part of his show was storytelling.

"I was walking down a country road, taking the cows to pasture," Mooney would reminisce, "when my toe hit something in the dust. I bent over to see what it was and I picked up an old pocketknife. I tried to open it with my fingers but I wasn't strong enough so I used my teeth to pry open its stubborn, rusty blade. I was so proud of my new find that I quickly hunted for a piece of wood to whittle . . . and I've been whittlin' ever since."

The story is true. Mooney inherited the chore of walking the cows to pasture at age five. In Switzerland, homeland of his parents, it was the custom for a young lad to gather his neighbors' cows and herd them into the hills for good grazing. The boy remained with the animals an entire season, caring for them and milking them twice daily. At season's end the youngster returned with the herd and the many pounds of cheese that he had made from the cows' milk. Each neighbor received the cheese produced by his cow, minus a token chunk to the young cheesemaker.

And so it was with Mooney Warther, except that he returned the cows every afternoon, just in time for the neighbors to do their own milking, and he was paid with cash and not cheese. Mooney's was a necessary chore. His Swiss neighbors needed someone to take their cows to the country (since there was no pasture land in town) and Mooney's impoverished family needed the money.

Life in America in the late nineteenth century was not comfortable for the Warthers. But they were not alone. Poverty surrounded them in their Swiss settlement of Dover, Ohio in Tuscarawas County. Like so many other Swiss who had been convinced to leave their native country for a new life, perhaps a better life in America, Godfrey and Anna Warther left their home in Tune, Switzerland in 1883 and sailed to America. With them they brought their two children, a daughter whose name has been forgotten with time, and an infant son, Fred. The family first settled in Port Washington, about fifteen miles southwest of Dover, where Godfrey found work in an Ohio coal mine. Shortly after their arrival, Anna gave birth to a third child, Jacob. The joy of Jacob's birth, however, was coupled with sorrow, as their young daughter did not survive the journey.

Anna and Godfrey Warther struggled to make a home and a life in the new world. Godfrey was an impressionable man. He was restless, often gruff and difficult to please and he was never satisfied with his job in the coal mine. It didn't provide enough money, for one thing, and the work was dangerous and filthy. About 1884 Godfrey heard that the Hanna Blast Furnace in Dover was hiring men and without hesitation he packed a wagon and moved his family to the larger town. Anna didn't mind. She looked forward to the Swiss immigrants in Dover who might ease her occasional pangs of homesickness and she hoped that a different job might improve Godfrey's disposition. The move was a welcomed change.

German settlers founded Dover in 1807 and by 1860 it was the fastest growing city in the country with a population of about ten thousand persons. At the turn of the century, twenty-six passenger trains stopped in Dover on a daily schedule and the Erie Canal ran through the city and added to the prosperity. Dover was so indebted to the Erie Canal that while the waterway was in service the city was called Canal Dover. In 1915, after the railroad made the canal obsolete, Canal was dropped from the name.

The Warthers bought a log cabin about one mile east of town on what is now known as Black Snake Hill. Godfrey had a long walk to the blast furnace, but that kept him healthy and he didn't mind. His new job paid better than the coal mine — ninety-nine cents a day for twelve hours a day — and the work wasn't so dangerous. However, his income was barely sufficient to provide for a family that would soon include a third son.

On October 30, 1885, Ernest was born to Anna and Godfrey Warther. Unlike their first three children, Ernest was blonde haired and light-complexioned and they jokingly called him "the missing link."

Not long after Ernest's birth, for reasons unknown, Godfrey moved his family to the opposite side of Dover, on Red Hill. There he found a hut-like home tucked into the rolling countryside just on the outskirts of town. It was a perfect setting for a growing family, but Godfrey wouldn't live long enough to know it. That next year Anna gave birth to Mary, and after three sons, Anna and Godfrey were thrilled for a daughter. Mary quieted the lingering grief from the death of their first daughter and the infant's good health was a comfort to her parents. About a year later, however, in 1888, the joy of life was again interrupted by the sorrow of death when Godfrey died unexpectedly of natural causes. He wasn't yet 30 and his death occurred just weeks prior to the birth of his last child, Anna.

With five children to provide for and no husband to
support them, Anna Warther's future was bleak.
Townspeople urged her to put the children up for adoption or
at least send them to a nearby children's home, but she
would hear nothing of it. She was a frail woman, Anna
Warther, but she was strong-willed and proud and
determined to earn her family's keep. She would *not*
abandon her children.

In town, Anna found work as a washerwoman for fifty
cents a day. And on Red Hill she cultivated a large garden
from which she sold vegetables and saved what she couldn't
sell for her children. Later, she became a midwife, and a good
one, so that every doctor in the area sought her services.
From these odd jobs she earned only a meager living but her
Swiss heritage had taught her thriftiness and her family
would survive. Her children would have clothes to wear —
she'd sew for them; they'd at least have bread to eat — she'd
get flour from John Wendling, a neighbor who worked at the
flour mill; and they'd have milk to drink from the family cow.
The Warther children would not know luxury, but they
would be together.

Mother Warther, or Muti Warther as she was called by the
Swiss, was an optimistic woman who believed that hard
work was the key to a good life. For her it was. It made no
difference that it was a poor life. She was a loving woman
who was loved. Most people in Dover knew Muti Warther,
either as a neighbor, a washerwoman or a midwife, and
many of them wanted to help her family. While the Warthers
lived on Red Hill, for example, the Wendlings fixed coffee
cake for them every Saturday evening, and that became an
anticipated treat. Many people gave the children hand-me-
downs that Muti was grateful to accept. And people were
always eager to buy vegetables from Muti Warther's
sprawling garden.

If the Warther children knew they were poor, it didn't

bother them. They didn't see wealth, so they didn't miss it. They loved living in the country, but eventually they'd move into a more convenient home in town. On Red Hill they slept on cornhusk matresses and found the sawdust floor to be just the thing for inviting the pigs and chickens inside when mother was away working. Fred, Jake and Ernest were comedians and they enjoyed entertaining their younger sisters, making them laugh at silly games or cry in fright at the sight of a harmless black snake. Of course, the boys also had to work, feeding the animals, weeding the garden and milking the cow, but they didn't mind. They sensed their responsibilities in a home without a man, in a time when a man was necessary.

On many occasions the children accompanied Muti when she went into town. One Christmas eve, Muti had to deliver wash, and so she bundled up her five youngsters for an evening's walk. Outside it was barely light and a crunchy snow covered Red Hill as they walked toward the flickering lights of Dover. It was a beautiful night. The air was biting, but not bitter, and thoughts of Santa Claus kept the children all the warmer. Halfway down the hillside, just as they finished singing Silent Night, Muti told the children to continue without her as she had forgotten something at home. She would catch up with them in town.

Later that evening, after the snow had fallen ankle deep and the night air was blowing colder, mother and children returned home, tired but warm with Christmas spirit. And just as they had hoped, Santa Claus had arrived. He had left clothes for each of them, plus a large sack of rock candy and five oranges. Indeed, it was a merry Christmas; one of many.

By the mid-1890s the Warther family had moved off Red Hill. Although they missed the country, it was more practical to live in town where Muti found most of her work and the children could attend school. They moved into a small, red brick home that faced Factory Street (now

Tuscarawas Avenue) on the edge of Dover's Swiss settlement. Just a few streets west were the Germans and below the Germans, the Italians. The three settlements did not always mix socially, but they respected each other's right to life in America.

The house on Factory Street was small for the Warther family and eventually they moved into a larger home in the heart of the Swiss settlement. There Muti had room for boarders (who provided extra income) and ample land to plant a yielding garden plus space for the boys to build a workshop near the rear of the lot. Their new home cost $1,700 and was quickly paid for through the efforts of Muti and her children. Muti would live in the home until she died in 1938.

As Muti's boys matured, they were anxious to work. It troubled them to watch their mother at work practically every waking moment, and while she never complained, they wanted to lighten her burden both physically and financially. Fred and Jake were mechanically inclined and before they were teenagers they sought odd jobs, particularly repair work. As their skills became known throughout Dover, the boys were kept continuously busy in their shop.

Even Ernest, who turned five in 1890, was eager to work. He was too young to help his brothers, however, but he was just the right age for herding cattle. Ernest was a country boy. He responded to the open land; the rolling hills of Tuscarawas County. It was home to him. Beginning in April of 1890 Ernest anxiously woke early every morning, jumped into his overalls and T-shirt, ruffled his curly blonde hair and ran off to gather the neighbor's cows. Rarely did he wear shoes. He didn't always have shoes to wear, of course, but he preferred bare feet and in later years he liked to think of himself as another Huckleberry Finn.

Every morning Ernest followed the same route to gather the cows; usually about a dozen. When the Swiss spotted him coming down the dusty road, they would call to him in a slang farm name that sounded like "moo-nay" and meant "bull of the herd." Ernest's non-Swiss friends had trouble pronouncing the word and it was quickly Anglicized to Mooney, a nickname that stuck for life.

It would take Mooney about an hour to gather the cows and walk them to the pasture land. A mile out of town, just below Red Hill, there was a major intersection where Mooney Warther grazed his herd. Third Street crossed the railroad tracks and the clear water of Sugar Creek before it was intersected by Fisher's Road to the south and Salt Well Road to the north. Third Street then turned into Red Hill Road.

When Mooney wanted to daydream and watch steam locomotives puff clouds of smoke into a clear blue sky, he'd graze the cows near the tracks. But when the grass was low there, he might take them to Fisher's Road or Salt Well Road where he could swim in adjacent Sugar Creek. Or, when he felt lonely, he'd continue up Red Hill and visit the men who fired kilns at the local brickyard. Mooney would graze the cows all morning and most of the afternoon and return them just before dinner. Once every month Mooney would collect his earnings of $1.25 and proudly present the money to his mother to help support the family. Some days Mooney was allowed to spend a penny for peanuts or a bag of rock candy and on the day the Spanish-American War ended, Muti allowed him fifteen cents for a bunch of firecrackers. That was a celebration!

Occasionally Mooney's brothers and his friends, Charlie Grunder, Dave Sylvan and Dave's half-brother, Herm Rieker, would tag along to the cow pastures. And when that happened there was no telling what mischief the gang might create. They knew how to entertain themselves! As the youngest, Herm was usually left to watch the cows while the others swam in Sugar Creek. But Herm didn't mind; he was

happy just being one of the gang. Down along the creek bank
Mooney and the older boys had hung a long rope from an elm
that branched over Sugar Creek. They'd swing over the
creek and drop into the cool, shallow water, enthusiastically
laughing and splashing. One day while the others were
swimming, Fred tied knots in their clothes. Later, his
buddies evened the score when they threw Fred, clothes and
all, into chilly Sugar Creek.

When the boys weren't swimming they were target
shooting or catching snakes. One afternoon they caught
thirty-one black snakes, and freed all of them except one that
Mooney hung from a tree branch. A few days later he and
Fred returned to the tree and found the snake still hanging
there, alive! "If he's lived this long," Mooney told his
brother, "he deserves to be free," and Mooney put the reptile
back on the ground. Mooney was intrigued by snakes and
while he was a boy he usually carried a black snake in his
pocket, just to have a pet and occasionally to scare a girl.

Most days Mooney herded the cows alone. It was on such a
day that he discovered the rusty pocketknife and thereafter
he rarely spent an idle moment. The young lad sharpened
the rusty knife blade and passed his cow-watching days
whittling sticks and bones. "After I found that knife,"
Mooney used to explain, "I found a wooden sign. I was too
young to read what the sign said and before long no one else
could read it either, because I'd whittled it to pieces." In the
beginning Mooney whittled spears and arrows and small
boats that he floated in the nearby creek. One morning
Mooney had carved a waterwheel when a doctor, returning
from a country call near Red Hill, stopped to see what the
young boy was doing. After examining the carvings, the
doctor told Mooney, "You're going to make something of
yourself one day, young man. Your carvings are excellent."
Mooney valued the doctor's compliment and it encouraged
him to continue whittling.

On the few occasions that Mooney tired of whittling, he
turned to fishing to ward off loneliness. He would graze the
cows along the lush creek banks and toss a line into the still
Sugar Creek. Usually, he didn't catch a thing and when he
returned to town with his fishing pole over his shoulder and
an empty stringer dangling from his hand, the neighbors
teased him about being a poor fisherman. "Feeding the fish
again?" they'd chide. Countless times Mooney was laughed
at until finally he decided to get the best laugh. Luck wasn't
with him on this particular day and the fish weren't biting.
But rather than return with a fishless stringer, Mooney
found a piece of plywood along the creek bank and carved
two slender fish. Then, he took a chunk of coal from along
the railroad tracks and drew in eyes, fins and tails. That
afternoon, when he returned the cows, there was nothing but
astonishment on the faces of his critics. Mooney's mother
was working in her garden and she also was surprised to see
her youngest son toss his catch into her wash bucket.
Quickly she went to clean the fish for the evening's meal but
when she picked up the chunks of wood she joined in
Mooney's laughter. It was the first of many practical jokes
that Mooney Warther would play in his lifetime.

Rarely a day passed when Mooney didn't take out his
rusty pocketknife and practice whittling. He could whittle a
variety of trinkets but for weeks he tried to copy a hobo
whom he once watched perform an incredible task with a
knife. Mooney was at the brickyard one afternoon when the
old gentleman made a few slices in a chunk of wood about
the size of a man's middle finger. Then the hobo split the
wood along the slices and worked the finished product like a
pair of miniature pliers. Mooney wanted to master the task
but he wasn't able to do it. The hobo was gone and Mooney
was left to discover the trick himself. He practiced diligently
but his wood was too brittle and it splintered when he tried to
split the pliers. Finally, after Mooney used a piece of wood

from the bottom of an old bucket, he mastered the trick. Immediately he collected every bucket in the neighborhood for he felt certain the pliers could only be cut from basswood. Later he learned that other woods were just as good and he produced hundreds of tiny pliers and gave them to his friends and family.

By the time he was ten, Mooney Warther had a following of friends who depended on him for a variety of functions. Often they needed someone to build them a wagon, which Mooney accomplished with an orange crate and a set of old baby buggy wheels. Sometimes they needed their bikes fixed and Mooney always knew how to make them roll again. But also they depended on him for entertainment. Youngsters, some older than Mooney, sat for hours and watched him cut wooden pliers and listened to his stories. Before long Mooney could fashion three pairs of pliers, all connected and out of the same chunk of wood, and then five pairs and seven pairs and eventually, in 1913, he cut his famous Plier Tree with 511 tiny pairs of pliers in one block of walnut.

Whittling pliers and other trinkets was fine for entertaining children or passing time in the cow pasture, but Mooney's talent demanded more of a challenge. He didn't want to be a whittler. "Whittlin' is when you sit in front of a store all day long, whittlin' and whittlin' on a stick of wood with your knife and never accomplishing anything but a pile of shavings. But carving, that's when you produce something more important than shavings," Mooney philosophized later in life. Mooney Warther, before he was a teenager, needed to be a carver.

Identifying an important project to carve was not difficult for young Mooney. He had started school at the age of six (during the winter months only) but quit after the second grade. He had too many responsibilities at home and, besides, Mooney didn't like the confinements of a school room. However, he loved education and was a fast learner.

Mooney devoted a part of his life to educating himself and those around him. He taught himself to read and write and he was especially fond of reading about Abraham Lincoln, his idol. In maturity Mooney would say, "I amounted to something because I read. I went through the second grade and attended the same school Abe Lincoln did. Everything I've done has been way ahead of what I ever dreamed of. I never expected my hobby to lead to all of this (referring to his museum of priceless carvings), but I would rather have written the Gettysburg Address than anything else in the world." It's understandable why Mooney carved many items in honor of America's sixteenth president.

One of Mooney's first tributes to Lincoln was begun when his hand and knife blade were eager to quit whittling. It was a cane. At the top of the cane, in walnut, Mooney sculpted a bust of Lincoln. At the opposite end of the cane, he cut a cagelike basket and inside it he left a loose wooden ball that was never touched by human hands, not even while it was being carved. How he managed to carve the tiny, perfectly round ball through the basket is among the wonders of Mooney Warther.

Not long after the turn of the century, when Mooney was still a teenager but a more disciplined carver, he cut a wall plaque in honor of Lincoln. At the top he carved an eagle and on the plaque he inscribed the words of Lincoln's lengthy favorite poem, *Oh, Why Should The Spirit of Mortal Be Proud?* Later, when Mooney was twenty-four, he read about Lincoln's letter to Mrs. Lydia Bixby who had lost five sons in the Civil War, and he carved a second plaque that included the letter.

About the time Mooney outgrew whittling, he also outgrew taking the cows to pasture. Another Swiss boy took over Mooney's chore and at age fourteen Mooney went to work at the American Sheet and Tin Plate Co. His first job was bundling scrap iron but in time he worked his way to

shearman. The mill, on South Factory Street adjacent to the
Tuscarawas River and opposite the railroad tracks, was
about one mile from Mooney's home. The mill was
uncomfortably hot and that made the work more difficult,
particularly for a teenager who weighed barely eighty
pounds. But Mooney was strong and eager and working in
the mill meant more money for his family. It was worth the
effort, he thought. Fred and Jake were providing their
shares of the family's welfare through their successful repair
business and the girls were busy with the garden and house
plus picking up after the boarders. Muti was busy canning
and selling vegetables when she wasn't at the side of a
doctor or aiding a young mother with her newborn. So
Mooney was impatient about his obligations and, at the
time, the mill was his only answer.

While the Warther boys were gentlemen, kind, considerate
and dedicated to their mother, they were also boys.
Occasionally they got into trouble, though it was never
anything serious. Mooney was usually the instigator. Once,
out in the workshop behind their home, Mooney carved a
model of the American battleship, the *Kearsarge*. The
Kearsarge was the flagship of the North American fleet and
Mooney had read about it when the ship was launched in
early 1898. He was proud of the model and enthusiastic
about showing the neighborhood gang the ship's cannon
which fired .22 blanks. However, the cannon made such a
bang and scared so many people that the police finally told
Mooney not to fire it.

At Halloween Mooney had a delightful time. He used to
attach a small weight, the size of a sinker, to the end of a
string. He'd then tack the other end of the string above a
window so that the weight hung in front of the glass. Then,
with a second string tied to the weight and stretched into the
bushes where he was hiding, Mooney gently pulled the
string and tapped the weight against the window. When

someone from inside sought out the eerie sound, he'd quickly pull the string taut to conceal the weight. Mooney was devilish and he enjoyed a harmless laugh. Occasionally, though, he got caught. One Halloween he used an oversized weight and in his excitement he shattered a window. That time he wasn't only caught, but he also paid for the glass!

Given a chance to run, however, Mooney rarely got caught. He was small, always in excellent physical condition, and fast. One of his mischievous activities was called The Farmer's Chase. The idea was to steal fruit from a farmer's orchard while the farmer was watching. In fact, if the farmer didn't give chase, the game had failed. One day Mooney and a friend were on Red Hill when they decided to steal some apples. The farmer spotted them and fell for the game. He chased the boys for more than a mile into the thick woods above the Salt Well Road. There they eluded him. Mooney and his pal sat under a large birch tree and ate their apples, laughing breathlessly between bites. After they had finished eating and were rested, Mooney took out his knife and carved into the tree — "The End of a Farmer's Chase, 1903." Mooney carved the letters very small so as the tree grew and the words expanded they would still be readable. For many years thereafter Mooney returned to that tree for a nostalgic chuckle.

In 1906 Mooney turned twenty-one and marked his seventh year in the steel mill where he was now making about three dollars a day. As did his brothers, Mooney continued to give his earnings to his mother and she wisely spent what was necessary and saved the rest. For years Muti Warther had talked about returning to her homeland to visit her family and friends. And by 1906, after an absence of twenty-three years, she had saved sufficient money for the trip. At the time, Jake and Fred were too busy in their workshop to go abroad and the girls had to stay behind to tend the garden and look after the boarders. But the mill was temporarily out of work and so Mooney decided to join his mother, who was now fifty-six years old. In June, 1906, Muti and Mooney sailed for a seven week trip in the old country. Anna was as eager to see the family and friends who had all but forgotten her as Mooney was to visit Switzerland and meet the relatives whom he had only heard about from his mother.

To Mooney's delight, his relatives were just as eager to meet him. They spent hours listening to him talk about his life in America, his stories of herding the cows and his episodes in the mill. And they were astounded at young Mooney's grasp of life and particularly at his knowledge of history. In fact, he could teach them not only about America but also about their native land. He impressed his relatives one day with his narrative of the Castle Volkenstein, built in 1207, and they decided that he should have a chance to visit the place. That was a highlight for Mooney. Naturally he couldn't leave the castle without a souvenir, so he took a piece of wood from the foundation and carved a pair of triple pliers. His relatives marveled at his work and told Mooney that his hands resembled those of his paternal grandfather who had been a skilled Swiss cabinetmaker. Mooney wanted to know more about his ancestors and he was told that his father's father was a waif who had been left on the doorstep of a family named Von Warth. Shortly before they sailed to the new land, Mooney's father changed the name to Warther — it sounded more American.

In their return to America, Mooney and Muti sailed on *La Lorraine*, a French ship with a French-speaking crew. The trip seemed endless, especially for Mooney who couldn't wait to return to Dover and tell about his experiences in Switzerland. To pass the time he needed some wood so he approached the ship's carpenter. The Frenchman couldn't understand the American passenger, however, until Mooney opened his knife and motioned that he wanted to whittle.

The carpenter smiled and pointed to a pile of white pine and Mooney graciously cut the crewman seven pairs of pliers in one piece of wood. The carpenter was so impressed that he immediately showed his prize possession to the captain and the passengers and for the remainder of the trip Mooney had an unending supply of wood — and a crowd that demanded him to perform. Certainly he obliged!

Muti and Mooney found life unchanged when they returned to Dover in the late summer of 1906. Naturally everyone in the settlement wanted to hear the latest news from their homeland and so Muti organized a party. Several of the women brought housenpepper (rabbit) and baked hams for good eating and Mooney set the phonograph player on the front porch to provide the music. Muti and Mooney, of course, were the attractions that night, telling about a trip that would never be forgotten nor repeated by them.

The day after the party Muti returned to midwifing and her routine chores and Mooney went back to the mill where his unchallenging job helped replenish the family's savings. To satisfy his creativity, however, Mooney continued his avocation and he spent many hours working with his brothers in their workshop. For years one of Mooney's favorite projects was developing a process for tempering steel. An old Swiss who worked in the local blast furnace had taught Mooney the art of tempering when he was still a teenager. Mooney was intrigued. He had often been discouraged by knives that were difficult to grip and blades that wouldn't hold an edge. He decided one day to make his own knives and, in fact, he perfected the old Swiss' method. (Today the unique method is a closely guarded secret of the third generation of Warther knife makers.)

In 1907 Mooney made one of his first knives. He made the handle from soup bone and the blade from scrap metal that he obtained from the mill. For several years Mooney used his knives for his personal carving but he discovered that housewives also appreciated his fine cutlery. That's when Mooney decided to make paring knives during his leisure and sell them throughout Dover. In the evenings Mooney often joined Fred and Jake in their small workshop and the young carver filled his knife orders while his brothers worked on their projects.

It was during one of those evenings that Mooney heard the voice of a young girl coming from the direction of his mother's garden. He poked his head out the workshop door, his hands busy carving a knife handle, and he recognized Frieda Richard, a neighbor girl. She was wearing a print dress, with an apron about her tiny waist, and in Swiss she was asking Muti for instructions about the care of an infant. Frieda was several years younger than Mooney and lived just down the alley. She was always busy, it seemed, at least as busy as Mooney's sisters, and she rarely paid Mooney any attention. Once he tried to scare her with a black snake, but she wasn't frightened or amused. And now, as she passed him enroute to her home, Frieda Richard was unyielding. Mooney returned to his knives.

Chapter Two

Frieda

At five o'clock on any given morning in the years immediately following the turn of the twentieth century, Frieda Richard, barely a teenager, would be awakened by the interfering cry of a hungry baby. Without hesitation the young girl would throw back her quilt and tend to the infant who was one of her twelve brothers and sisters. As the second oldest child and the eldest daughter of Frederick and Lena Richard it was Frieda's responsibility to care for the children and perform many of the household chores.

After the baby was satisfied and back to sleep, and providing it wasn't Sunday when the family would attend church, Frieda would quietly dress and hurry downstairs to the kitchen. She had to light the coal stove and prepare for a long day of baking. Her mother would already be in the kitchen fixing breakfast for the family and her father would usually be stepping out the back door on his way to a job at the local blast furnace. Frieda's parents were hard working Swiss who believed in the ways of the old country and they set a good example for their offspring. Frederick was stern and stubborn and often he appeared sour, but he was an honest man and a good provider. Lena was more gentle, but often just as stern, and she required more of Frieda than most mothers would of a teenaged daughter. Frieda didn't resent her responsibilities despite the restrictions they imposed. As did most Swiss children of the time, Frieda understood her family role and accepted it proudly and willingly. She knew she was loved and appreciated and that was her security.

Most mornings, Frieda and Lena worked side by side in the kitchen and talked about the old days when they had lived in Switzerland. It hadn't been so long before that Frieda couldn't remember. They lived with Grandma and Grandpa Christian, Lena's parents, and a dwarf uncle who was captured and later released by the Barnum and Bailey Circus. Work was scarce in Switzerland and Frederick was usually without a job. It depressed him when he wasn't able to provide for his family and as a result he was not happy. Young men Frederick's age were encouraged to seek new lives in different lands and in 1893 Frederick decided, though unwantingly, that if he were to make a better life for himself, his wife and his children, it would have to be in America. They sailed on the next boat.

Upon arrival in America Frederick settled his family in Stonecreek, about sixteen miles southeast of Canal Dover and not far from Port Washington. Several other Swiss families who had come over on the same boat established their homes in the country setting and the men joined the work force at the local coal mine. Despite the opportunities America provided, it was still not a pleasant time for these Swiss immigrants. They sustained sufferings that only immigrants could understand. They left their native land and their loved ones for a dream of a better life, and they had no guarantee their dreams could ever be fulfilled. Of course, in America their dreams would at least have a chance, and so they persevered.

Frederick was thankful to at last have a job to support his family. He didn't mind that it was tedious work nor did he complain that the hours were long and the job was low paying. He was a man again. Lena Richard naturally knew the thriftiness of the Swiss and she found ways to manage their meager income so as to get the most from her husband's hard earned dollars. They wouldn't have plenty, but they would have enough, or at least they'd make do.

In time the Richards adjusted to their new land; their spirits swelled and they were proud to be living in America. Occasionally they suffered pangs of homesickness, but any thoughts of returning to their native country were quickly dismissed. Of course they missed their family but there were too many mouths to feed to save money for a trip home, and besides, there was always work in the mine and vacations were not practical.

To somewhat satisfy their longing for their homeland the Richards spent what time they could visiting other Swiss families who had settled in the area. It was comforting to share their new lives with friends who could understand their feelings and it was also fortifying. An hour or two of talking about the hard times in Switzerland was enough to re-charge their dreams of a better life in America.

Of course there were days when they felt certain their better lives would forever remain dreams. One Sunday in 1896 Frederick and his family and some friends from Canal Dover were hiking out near the coal mine where Frederick worked. As they approached the mine, the Richard's playful German shepherd started acting in a peculiar manner, barking and howling furiously. The dog jumped on Frederick with enough force to knock him to the ground and just as Frederick was about to swat the dog the earth started to tremble. Within seconds the mine collapsed in a cloud of smoke.

Without a coal mine there was no work, of course, and once again Frederick Richard was without a job. Frieda by this time was six years old and there were three other children in the family. A fifth child was expected within a month. Fortunately Frederick was a self-starter and he didn't hesitate to take advantage of his opportunities. He packed his family's belongings and moved to Dover where he had heard the Hanna Blast Furnace was in need of men.

In Dover's Swiss settlement, Frederick found a home in an alley between Third and Fourth Streets. It was small, too small for his large family, but it would have to do. Frederick knew his job in the blast furnace would barely pay enough money to support his multiplying family and there would be little money left to save for a larger home. In Switzerland, Frederick was a skilled carpenter and so he let it be known in town that he was available to do odd jobs. In no time Frederick had more jobs than he could possibly accomplish, working after his twelve-hour shift at the blast furnace and on Saturdays. Of course he never worked on Sundays.

Even with the extra money, Frederick found it difficult to provide for his wife and children, but eventually they became comfortable in the Swiss settlement. Lena kept a garden behind their home and she knew most of the Swiss families in the area, though she had little time for socializing. The children had many neighborhood playmates but, as was the tradition, the children also worked. The boys took charge of pumping and carrying well water and milking the family cow. As they grew older and more capable they helped their father with his odd jobs. The girls helped Lena with the wash and in the garden but most other household duties, including baking, were left to Frieda.

Every day, except Sunday, Frieda baked fifteen loaves of bread and twenty-five dozen cookies from six in the morning through late afternoon. Then, before dinner, she peddled her baked goods, along with her mother's vegetables, in season. On one such afternoon Frieda met Mooney Warther. She spotted him down an alley, barefoot and curly haired, herding several cows back from the pasture land. Mooney was five years older than Frieda but his mother and Lena were close friends and Frieda had often heard about Muti Warther's young boy. Though he had never met her, on this particular day Mooney had a black snake in his pocket and when Frieda said hello to him he used the snake to scare her. To Mooney's surprise, Frieda was not frightened. And when he saw she didn't think his joke was funny, he quickly tucked away the snake and continued following his herd. Frieda Richard was not to be teased. In fact, when it was necessary she could protect herself. Once Frieda was walking home from church when two boys ran up on either side of her and started making fun of her hat and calling her names. Frieda took their jeers in stride but only for a while. With one quick movement she grabbed her hat pin and stuck one of the pests in his thigh. Frieda was seldom bothered after that!

After a seventh child was born to Frederick and Lena they were compelled to find a larger home. None of the available houses in the settlement were large enough and so Frederick rented a home on Second Street, just a few blocks east of the settlement. Several of the children were enrolled in Oak Grove School (now Dover High School) which was just a short walk from their home. Frieda had started school there shortly after her family moved to Dover but by the time she was thirteen and through the sixth grade there were eight children in her family and Lena needed her at home full-time. Girls were allowed to quit school after the sixth grade then, since they didn't need much education just to become mothers and housewives.

Frieda was disappointed about quitting school. She enjoyed learning and she was a good student but she understood why she couldn't continue. After she quit she occasionally studied with her younger brothers and sisters and she taught herself through the eighth grade. High school was too difficult for her to grasp on her own, and besides, there was just no time for studying. Frieda's yearning to learn would not escape her, however, and she would satisfy it in later years.

There wasn't much fun in life for a teenager like Frieda

Richard. Even after dinner her work day was not complete
until she helped bathe the younger children and put them to
bed. And by eight o'clock, Frieda was eager to get to bed
herself. She considered her work her contribution to her
family's dream for a better life and she couldn't let fun
interfere. As a result, work became a way of life for Frieda,
just as it had for her mother and for most other Swiss
women.

In Frieda's late teens, when several of the younger
children were capable enough to help ease her workload, she
began attending Christian Endeavor, a youth program
sponsored by St. John's Evangelical Church where most
Swiss families attended services every Sunday. On Sunday
evenings the youth were brought together for Christian
fellowship and recreation. It was a splendid means for boys
to meet girls and vice versa and many of the frivolous
romances of Christian Endeavor were later solemnized in
marriage.

Among the available young men at Christian Endeavor
during the early 1900s was Mooney Warther. Frieda
recognized him one Sunday evening and remembered the
time he tried to scare her with a black snake. She saw little of
him after her family moved out of the settlement but she
often heard about him from her mother who remained
friends with Muti Warther. Frieda was surprised when
Mooney approached her and asked her to join him on a walk.
"I don't know any of the other girls here but I know you," he
said shyly. Cautiously Frieda accepted Mooney's invitation
and walked with him out over Dover Hill, which is about
three miles from the church. That evening was the first of
many walks with Mooney Warther as Frieda discovered she
liked Muti Warther's young boy. She found it difficult to
forgive him for trying to scare her that day, but Mooney's
envious sense of humor was one Frieda could tolerate and

enjoy. Best of all, Mooney Warther was dependable. And, it appeared that he liked her.

Suddenly Frieda found herself anticipating Christian Endeavor. Before, Sunday had always meant a day of rest, but now it meant much more. Frieda could complete a week's batch of baking with an ease she never before recognized. She was in love.

Mooney Warther must have felt that love, too. For he never missed a session at Christian Endeavor after that Sunday night walk with Frieda Richard. He was always there and always impatient for the session to end so he could be with Frieda. During the summer months they bought ice cream cones and walked out through the country; and then, when it turned cold, they walked directly to Frieda's for the warmth of a fire and a game of Flinch. The young couple had more in common than just their heritage. They were both eager to learn and they wanted nothing more than a simple life. Mooney Warther was good for Frieda Richard. He was fun for her. And she was good for him — she understood him.

It was inevitable that Mooney would ask Frieda to marry him. He asked her one evening in 1910 when she was twenty and Mooney, twenty-four. Frieda didn't know how to respond at first; yes, she wanted to marry him but there was still so much to be done at home. The Richards were now renting a country home on Dover Avenue and with so many children Lena still depended on her eldest daughter. Hesitantly Frieda told her mother of Mooney's proposal. "You're old enough to make your own decision," Lena said in a manner that was not intended to persuade or discourage her daughter from marrying. Frieda, for one of the few times in her life, was overwhelmed with joy. She promised her mother that even after she married Mooney she would return home every day and help with the chores. One Sunday not long thereafter, Frieda Richard became Frieda Warther in a ceremony at St. John's Evangelical Church. Having no time for a wedding trip — both Mooney and Frieda had to work the next day — they hiked out over Dover Hill where their romance had begun.

Mooney and Frieda lived with Muti Warther after they were married since she had more room on Fifth Street than did Lena Richard. And every morning, Frieda rose with the sun, made breakfast for the Boss, as she referred to Mooney, and then walked the mile-and-a-half to her parents' home where she baked and cared for the children. This practice continued for about one year. The Richards' last child, Eddie, was born on January 24, 1911 and Frieda was there to care for him. But nine months to the day later, Frieda Warther was at home on Fifth Street; Muti Warther was at her side, and she gave birth to a son, Tom. After the birth of her own child, Frieda returned home only occasionally, and then mostly for social visits.

Mooney and Frieda were anxious to build their own home. Muti Warther would have been content to have them live with her, but they wanted to live in the country. Frieda had become accustomed to country life while her family lived on Dover Avenue and Mooney had never forgotten his years on Red Hill. Mooney had been saving money from his knife business to buy a piece of land that he and Frieda wanted just north of Dover. There was about an acre there that sat above the outmoded millstream that ran parallel to the adjacent railroad tracks. Mooney and Frieda thought it would be perfect for their home. The land was elevated just enough to give them a picturesque view of a portion of the Tuscarawas Valley, which now meant so much to them. And, of course, it would be a motivating spot for a young carver of steam locomotives.

The newlyweds were out for a walk one Sunday, as was their habit, and they met the owner of the land they hoped to buy.

"It'll cost you $450," the man said, and Mooney replied, "We'll take it."

"Good — come back tomorrow," the owner explained, "Today is Sunday. Can't do business on Sunday."

In the fall of 1912, Mooney and Frieda moved into their own two-story, red brick home. Behind their home they included a workshop, ten feet by twelve feet, and a garden. The lot required landscaping but the new owners had many ideas that they would cultivate in the years to come. Unlike their parents, Mooney and Frieda Warther never had to move. They were settled, and they would remain for life at 331 Karl Avenue.

Chapter Three

Apprenticeship

One June afternoon in 1913, twelve year old Don Frary crept along the towpath that ran just below Mooney Warther's back yard on Karl Avenue. He was an Indian, or pretending to be one and he was spying on a cowboy camp that was threatening his tribe of warriors. The cowboys, numbering a half-dozen and ranging in age from six to twelve, were huddled in a corner of the outmoded Calico Ditch, and young Don was planning a surprise attack. Slowly, quietly he crouched below the milkweeds and peered from behind the bushes that bordered Mooney Warther's property. As soon as he could position himself on the upper flank of the cowboys he'd signal his tribe to attack from below. All at once Don was startled by the ring of a "whooooooo-peeeeee" from behind him. He spun around and spotted Mooney Warther, shoulders bent forward, face raised to the sky, knees pumping and his hand covering his mouth to the rhythm of a war chant. Don Frary knew about Mooney Warther but he'd never met the idol of the neighborhood and this introduction was one he'd never forget.

Mooney laughed and then invited the frightened young warrior to join him on a bench just outside his workshop. Mooney had been sitting there most of the afternoon carving a piece of black walnut and watching the cowboys and Indians.

Cautiously Don approached the mysterious Mooney.

"Whatcha doin'?" he asked, forgetting about the threatening cowboys.

"Carvin' a plier tree," Mooney explained. Mooney had read that a man once cut one hundred twenty-seven pairs of tiny pliers into a piece of wood twenty-four inches long and he intended to better that record. It was a meaningless project, Mooney agreed, but it had to be done. He cut a piece of black walnut thirteen inches long, three-quarters of an inch wide and five-eighths of an inch thick. Mathematically Mooney figured he could cut five hundred eleven pairs of pliers into the block of wood and when he opened the pliers they would form a tree-like object.

"Think I can do it?" Mooney asked the crew of youngsters that had now abandoned their game and joined Don Frary.

"Sure you can!" shouted his admirers.

Every day between June 24 and August 28 Mooney spent six to eight hours working on this project which he called the Master Piece of Tongs. Most days his group of young friends gathered around his bench to watch and absorb Mooney's folklore. Finally, after thirty-one thousand cuts, Mooney carefully opened each tiny pair of pliers until, indeed, they formed a tree. It was an unbelievable feat that Ripley showed at the Century of Progress in Chicago in 1933. And then, for fourteen years the tree was displayed at the Ohio State museum in Columbus. (Today, the Plier Tree is in the Warther Museum in Dover along with Mooney's collection of steam locomotives and other memorabilia.)

It never took long for Mooney Warther to draw a crowd, particularly when there were youngsters around. Often they would spot him carving near his shop or working in the garden but usually his voice gave away his presence. No one has ever explained Mooney Warther's loud voice. In jest, some said he developed it as a boy when he sang to his cows and needed to be heard over the chugging locomotives. But

Mooney's voice was solid; a naturally good voice for a showman: it was audible a block away and it was magnetic.

Through the 1960s there was always a group of boys and girls that could be called Warther's neighborhood gang. The manners and attitudes of the gangs, of course, changed with the times. After television became popular in the early 1950s, children weren't so easily entertained, not even by Mooney Warther. But prior to that era, youngsters looked beyond their living rooms for fun and they found it in Mooney Warther's back yard.

A few years after Mooney and Frieda settled in their new home, they purchased an additional acre of land that included the Calico Ditch and expanded their backyard. A stream had once run through the ditch and powered the Hardesty Flour Mill but when the mill closed its doors in 1901 the stream was drained. The ditch was named the Calico in 1842 when the man who built the ditch went bankrupt and had to pay for his labor with bolts of calico from his dry goods store.

Mooney bought the land to enhance his property and to create a playground for his children and their neighborhood friends. In 1916 Mooney moved his workshop to the rear of the lot and built an oversized sand box in its place. Below the sandbox in the Calico Ditch, Mooney built a merry-go-round and a teeter-totter and in 1920 he added the highlight of the playground: a tree swing. A towering elm once branched over the Calico Ditch and Mooney climbed it one morning and from the strongest limb hung a fifty-one foot cable and attached a wooden swing to the end of the cable. Then he built several jump-off platforms at various levels, one in front of the cave that he had built for the children to play in, another above it and a third up near the garden. The highest platform gave the rider a breathtaking ninety foot arc that spanned the ditch and overlooked the valley and cornfields below. Mooney's swing instantly became as famous as his pliers and his voice and through the years youngsters and adults visited Warther's just for a sensational ride.

Many times, while the children waited their turns on the swing, they'd sit on the workbench in Mooney's shop and watch him carve. Mooney's skilled hands were spellbinding and the busiest of children would sit for hours and watch him work. While he carved, Mooney reminisced about the old days when he had herded the cows and his stories were better than fairy tales. Mooney knew everything, so the children thought, and no one ever doubted his word. Occasionally, when they asked, Mooney would teach his young friends how to whittle various trinkets but none of them ever became very adept. The most they could do was carve spears and arrows. One summer afternoon Mooney helped the gang carve spears and then he cut a large cross and hung it around the neck of Don Frary. Instead of playing an Indian, this time Don was a missionary and the rest of the gang pretended to be hostile natives. They escorted Don to the Calico Ditch and tied him to a post where they danced around him in movie-cannibal fashion. Mooney was amused by it all and his brother Jake was there to snap a photo of the scene.

Exciting as it was, however, even Mooney's back yard occasoinally bored a neighborhood gang. During the summer, particularly on hot, muggy afternoons, the youngsters would pester Mooney to take them to the swimming hole. Usually Mooney would oblige them as he was just as eager for a refreshing swim. Prior to the early 1930s, there weren't any girls in Mooney's gang, so they'd strip at the workshop and race across the railroad tracks to the secluded swimming hole at Sugar Creek. Mooney would take the lead, whooping and hollering through the cornfields and past the Do Drop Inn where he was careful not to disturb the hobos waiting to hop the next freight car.

"Don't bother them and they won't bother you," Mooney

would tell the gang, which usually included Don Frary, Hiner and Walter Richard, Chuck Mathias, and Lawrence Carmola and in later years Kenny Espenschied, Chester Kennedy, Bob and Johnny Meese and Tom and Jim Warther. Occasionally Mooney's brothers Fred and Jake would tag along.

They raced to see who could be first in the water and usually it was Mooney. The gang always did a lot of splashing and clowning at the swimming hole but Mooney also taught the boys to swim. Mooney was patient and very careful not to frighten the youngsters. He encouraged them to lie on their stomachs in shallow water where their fingertips could touch the muddy bottom of Sugar Creek. Then, with their legs directed toward the center of the creek, Mooney guided the young swimmers into the water. Slowly — and often this took days of practice — Mooney taught the children to kick their feet and paddle their hands underwater until eventually, one day, they started swimming. "Keep your head low and your mouth closed," he'd tell them, "or you'll drain the creek!"

Mooney and his gang cherished the swimming hole, which eventually they named The Elm, in honor of the big elm that they used as a diving platform and from which they hung a swing. They took time to keep the banks of The Elm clean and the water clear of debris and they made certain that newcomers to the swimming hole respected their refreshing spot. By the mid-1930s The Elm enjoyed great popularity. Many families in Dover would pack a picnic lunch and hike to The Elm for a Sunday afternoon swim. Of course, much to the chagrin of the Warther gang, everyone then had to wear swimming suits!

In the early years of Mooney Warther's career he'd take his gang on arrowhead expeditions in the bottom lands that bordered Sugar Creek. Various Indian tribes had once inhabited the land now turned into farms and their artifacts were obvious to the trained eyes of Mooney Warther. "Look for the sun's reflection in the flint and that's how you'll know if it's a real arrowhead," he would instruct his friends. During the plowing seasons, after the farmers had turned over deep chunks of earth, Mooney and company would scour the fields for Indian relics. Walter Richard, one of Frieda's younger brothers, always made certain he was available when Mooney was going arrowhead hunting. Mooney helped Walter find his first arrowhead in a pasture adjacent to Sugarcreek Road and Walter was so fond of it that he began an arrowhead collection that eventually won dozens of ribbons at fairs and other displays.

There were many collectors in Tuscarawas County and the arrowheads eventually became very scarce. However, Mooney believed that any young child who wanted an arrowhead ought to be able to find one. And so on the evenings prior to one of his expeditions he'd sneak to the nearby pasture land and plant an arrowhead for every member of his gang.

After Mooney had collected more than four thousand arrowheads he and Frieda decided to mount them in various interesting designs on hardboard. Mooney later used the mountings to cover the ceiling and walls of his workshop. A few of the arrowheads, those that Mooney valued most, were kept under glass on a table in the living room.

Mooney wasn't as sentimental about arrowheads, of course, as he was his carvings, but they meant more to him than a good knife. Once he discovered that a friend of his had an arrowhead that was the most perfect of its kind. The friend valued the arrowhead and Mooney knew it could never be purchased but he was determined to get it. A true collector never sells, Mooney knew, but he hunts, trades and gives away. With that in mind Mooney made two paring knives and then he fashioned an extraordinarily handsome hunting knife. The next rainy Sunday afternoon, when

Mooney knew a visitor would be most welcome, he walked to his friend's home for the strategic visit. At the opportune moment Mooney showed his paring knives to his friend's wife and when she liked them so well he gave her the set. Then, Mooney pulled out his hunting knife and his friend immediately offered to buy it. "It's not for sale," Mooney said, "but I'll trade it." And that evening Mooney returned home and placed another arrowhead under the glass top of his table.

No matter how many arrowheads there were to collect or how many children there were begging to go swimming, Mooney devoted most of his leisure hours to his carvings. For many years, dating back to when Mooney was a teenager, he had been thinking about a lifetime project that he might carve in wood. It was in 1913, about the time he carved the Plier Tree, that Mooney finally decided he would carve the Evolution of the Steam Engine. He was twenty-seven years old when he started the project and he wouldn't finish it until his sixty-eighth birthday in 1953.

It's not certain why Mooney decided to carve the Evolution of Transportation, as he first called it, but his decision never surprised anyone. He had fallen in love with steam locomotives at a very early age and as he matured he understood and appreciated the importance of those huge chunks of iron. "If it weren't for the steam engine," Mooney Warther used to say, "America would be many nations instead of one." And because of Mooney Warther, the importance of steam could never be forgotten in America. Mooney's dedication, in fact, outlived even the steam locomotives themselves.

During Mooney's teens he had carved many crude replicas of steam locomotives. However, none of these carvings were acceptable to him and while he stored several of them in his attic on Karl Avenue, the majority of them he used for firewood. Prior to 1913, in fact, when Mooney was a less disciplined carver, he had cut more than twenty engines and none of them exist today.

But on the first of December in 1913 Mooney decided he would scale his engines one-half inch to the foot. That would improve their appearance and put them on top of the fireplace rather than inside it. The scaled carvings required disciplined hands and thus, Mooney Warther's apprenticeship had ended.

In order for Mooney to make his carvings realistic, he decided to carve the locomotives in small sections and then piece them together. Some of the models would require as many as six thousand parts, most of them tiny and intricate and therefore difficult to carve. Mooney used ebony, walnut and ivory for the various parts and a very stable applewood for the framework which had to be perfectly straight. The applewood, however, was not aesthetically pleasing so Mooney collected mussel shells from the local river and covered the wood with pearl plating. Each engine wheel required fifty-four parts cut in ivory and ebony and for the bearings (so that the wheels would actually rotate) Mooney used an oily wood from the swamps of South America. Mooney remembered that when he was a boy herding his cows near the brickyard a hobo once told a machine operator that he wouldn't need to oil his machine had the machine been made of arguto wood. Mooney never forgot that name and since oil would stain ivory, it was important for him to use the oily wood in his models. Mooney, however, didn't know where to buy arguto wood and so he wrote to the Bureau of Information in Washington, D.C. and he was directed to a supplier. (The Warther carvings may run forever without oil. The DeWitt Clinton, oldest carving in the Evolution of the Steam Engine, is nearly sixty-five years old and it has never needed a drop of oil.)

Mooney had carelessly carved the DeWitt Clinton, the first locomotive of the New York Central, in 1910, but it wasn't acceptable for his collection. So on December 1, 1913 he started again and he completed the engine two months to the day later. The DeWitt Clinton, named in honor of the New York mayor, was built in 1831 and had a top speed of fifteen-miles-an-hour. Mooney's 1913 carving was so fine, in fact, that he gave it away not long after completing it. He carved the engine a third time in 1916 and then a final time in 1928, when he duplicated most of his collection. Amazingly, Mooney made two or three models of most of his locomotives. He loved the General, the great Civil War locomotive, and so he carved it four times. The 999, Empire State Express was such a challenge that he carved it six times.

After Mooney had decided on his project he was devoted to it. As soon as he finished one engine, he collected photographs for his next selection, and within weeks he would be carving again. The time required to carve an engine depended on the complexity of the engine and Mooney's free time from the mill. A few carvings, like Sir Isaac Newton's Proposed Locomotive of 1680 and Leonardo Da Vinci's Steam Engine of the fifteenth century were completed in a few days. But others, like the Pioneer of 1836, the Atlantic of 1904 and the Pacific of 1914 required four to six months carving time.

Mooney was meticulous about dates and he thought it important to record the number of hours he spent carving his engines. In 1915 he began a diary, the first of several. In addition to his carving time Mooney also listed the number of parts for each of his models and he inscribed appropriate thoughts about many of the locomotives. Even more interesting he used the diaries to highlight historic days and events. On the eleventh day of November in 1918 he wrote: "Mooney the whittler would not look at the engines or would he pick up a file to file a bone. It is the greatest day of all history and never will have an equal. He shot his musket till his shoulder was so sore that he got very little done the next day. What of it. E. Warther." And below his signature he wrote, "The Great War is over."

November 11, 1918 was not typical for Mooney, however. A normal day, in those early years of his carving career, went more like this: "Today is May 12, 1916. This was a busy day for old Mooney. Worked first turn at the mill, came home at 9, ate, changed clothes, fussed with children for a while, then hauled two wheel barrow loads of sod for two squares, made a chock stick, fixed a vacuum cleaner, lined up a knife, put a sight on a gun, put a handle on a hand grip and bored two stogey holders and then I was all in so I went down to Joe's and fetched a glass of beer." All of this was preceded by several hours of carving.

Most days Mooney carved an average of six hours and that was before or after a full turn at the mill, when the mill was operating. "Just walked back from Sugarcreek," Mooney wrote in late 1917. "The mill has been off for two weeks."

It was on December 1, 1917 that Mooney wrote, "Today it is four years that I started the Evolution of Transportation. Sixteen engines have been finished and now at 12:30 I will start on the General for the second time, the first (model) being at the Columbus (Ohio) state museum."

And on the final day of that year Mooney wrote, "That finishes up 1917, two years of keeping a record of just how I worked at the mill and used up my spare time. Now I will not keep talley [sic] any longer as it is too much bother. Yours truly, E. Warther."

However much of a bother it was, Mooney Warther couldn't resist a diary. It was as irresistible as a good story. He might miss a year or two but eventually he would get back to writing in his pocket-sized, leather-bound books. If Mooney had had his way, life would have been so simple. He would have been content to spend his days at home, entertaining the children, carving, making knives and

writing in his diary. But in those early days Mooney Warther
had a wife and five children to support. And while it was
getting less dependable every year, the mill was his primary
source of income. In time, though, Mooney Warther would
have his way.

Chapter Four

The Steel Mill

Few men worked harder than Mooney Warther. Ask anyone who knew him at the steel mill and he'll tell you — Mooney Warther could work the jobs of two men, and he often did. By 1899 Mooney had outgrown his cow-herding chores and so he white-lied himself (he was underage) into a job at the local steel mill. The mill had been established on South Factory Street in 1866 as the Dover Rolling Mill. For its first thirty years the mill was a faltering business, plagued by mismanagement and poor leadership. However, a year after Mooney was hired, the American Tin Plate Company and the American Sheet Steel Company, purchased the Dover Rolling Mill, renamed it the American Sheet and Tin Plate Company, and gave it new life. In a matter of months the new owners managed the mill to prosperity and eventually it became a branch of United States Steel.

The American Sheet and Tin Plate Company employed approximately one thousand two hundred men between 1900 and 1930 and its existence was vital not only to Dover but to Ohio's steel industry as well. Mooney was hired to bundle scrap iron and toss the bundles into gondola cars so that the scrap could be recycled. At best it was a menial task but it paid a dollar a day. Soon, though, as fourteen year old Mooney became known to the company foremen and they sensed his enthusiasm and dedication, he was promoted to the position of opener and paid $2.25 per day.

"To be an opener," Mooney used to explain, "you needed a strong back and a weak mind." And since Mooney Warther's mind was as unyielding as his back, he didn't remain long as an opener. Eventually he was promoted to hold-up, a less strenuous position at the same pay, and then finally, about 1910, he was raised to shearman, the top job on the line. Some days it paid as much as $15.00.

The American Sheet and Tin Plate Company produced sheet metal used to manufacture such things as buckets, roofing and automobiles. The process for producing sheet metal was not complicated but it was routine and physical. Bars of iron, shipped in by rail from Pittsburgh, were fired red hot in blazing furnaces and then rolled flat and stacked eight to twelve sheets high. The opener would bend over the stack of iron sheets and, using a pair of tongs, pass one sheet at a time to the shearman. The shearman, assisted by the hold-up, was responsible for accurately sizing the sheets to fill the mill's orders. With the exception of the shearman's, the jobs required little concentration but the bulky sheet iron and the intense heat made the work exhausting.

Mooney operated mill number ten, the largest on the line, and half of mill number nine. Fortunately for the men in Mooney's crew, they were stationed near the end of the plant where two large doors ushered in cool, fresh air on balmy days when the mill was hot and muggy. Although the heat bothered Mooney, it did not slow down his production. At five feet, seven inches tall and eventually about one hundred twenty-seven pounds, Mooney was one of the mill's smallest laborers. And yet, on most days, he sheared more than thirty thousand pounds of ten-gauge steel — more than any other employee. Mooney was conscientious about his job but he had an overpowering incentive: his carvings. Some days, particularly after 1913 when he began the Evolution of the

Steam Engine, Mooney sheared two sheets of steel concurrently so that he could fill his orders and return to his workshop to carve.

Besides being the mill's most productive employee, Mooney was also the most jocular fellow on the line. His good nature, combined with his speed and sincerity, made Mooney's crew the most envied of the plant and there were always several men waiting for a vacancy on mills nine-and-a-half and ten. For several years, Johnny Richard, Mooney's brother-in-law, was Mooney's hold-up. Mooney and Johnny had been friends for as long as Mooney had known Frieda and they enjoyed each other immensely. Johnny, unfortunately, was killed in service in World War I. His death was a great personal loss to Mooney. Johnny Richard could never be replaced in Mooney's eyes.

The opener in those early days was Tom Moore, Jr. of New Philadelphia, a Johnny Bull, who like his co-workers was inclined to having fun when it was appropriate. After the opener's job had been vacated on Mooney's crew, Tom told Mooney he wanted to join him and Mooney interceded with the foreman. Mooney had known Tom for several years as a steady, energetic worker and thought he was well suited for the grueling opener's spot.

After Johnny Richard's death, Mooney often shared memories of Johnny with Tom, and the two of them became better than casual friends. They worked closely and efficiently, the result of their compatible personalities. In the mornings Mooney and Tom clocked themselves enroute to the mill so that their bicycles would roll onto the lot at about the same moment. At lunch time, neither of the men went home to eat, preferring instead to carry their lunches and eat together in the fresh outdoors on a log that they had set up. In the cold months they'd eat in front of the fireplace in the plant. Lunch time was generally a lark for Mooney and Tom.

"What the hell kind of lunch did you bring today?" Tom

often chided when Mooney opened his lunch bucket. Mooney was health-conscious and knowledgeable about nutritional requirements. A meal for him often consisted of whole wheat bread dipped in olive oil, rolled oats, a bag of nuts and a couple of raw carrots. Tom, despite Mooney's prodding, preferred a more substantial lunch, topped off with a wedge of homemade pie or a hunk of chocolate cake.

Neither of the men overindulged in lunch as they were not preoccupied by food. They preferred to spend their lunch breaks on special projects, nonsense not excluded. Many of the millmen, like Boots Mizer, who had known Mooney for years, and Lawrence Carmola, who would eventually open a shoe repair store in Dover, expected Mooney to entertain them. Mooney never disappointed them. One day he asked if anyone had a nail for him to bite — he wanted to prove that his teeth were stronger than steel. For some reason it was against mill regulations to carry nails and so Mooney knew that no one would oblige him. He quickly picked a nail from his shirt pocket and carefully displayed it between two fingers. Then, he put the nail between his teeth and bit down furiously. After several seconds of grunting and shuddering, Mooney showed his crowd that he had indeed nearly bitten through the nail.

"It was the laughablest day you ever saw," Mooney would say for years thereafter and chuckle when he recalled the event. At the time, none of the millmen knew that Mooney had previously filed the eight penny almost in two and when he held it up for them to inspect his fingers concealed the indentations. Mooney was also known for nailing a man's lunch bucket to a workbench, nailing a pair of shoes to a wooden plank and replacing a piece of pie in a lunch pail with a wedge of wood. Lunch time was fun time.

Most days, however, Mooney's lunch periods were spent wisely. Once a week he collected the mill's discarded saw blades which he would later use in his knife-making business. On many days he carved trinkets as gifts for his friends and relatives. And before holidays he carved greeting cards and mailed them to friends throughout the country. One Christmas Mooney made Tom Moore a miniature plier tree enclosed in glass and for Tom's wedding he gave the bride three of his now famous kitchen knives.

Tom's lunch periods weren't spent quite so productively as Mooney's. Occasionally Tom watched Mooney carve a piece of a locomotive or a greeting card, but Tom had no patience for carving. Invariably he'd pester Mooney with the lyrics of an old Swiss song which he'd sing in his best baritone voice:

> I miss my Swiss,
> Hi-O the mountain tops
> A sailing we will go.
> I miss my Swiss,
> My Swiss miss misses me.

Tom generally ended his lunch periods out near the fence that separated the mill from Factory Street. There, on many occasions, Tom's girlfriends visited him and he revelled in their company. But as Tom entertained the girls he riled Mooney.

"Get away from that boy and let him get back to work," Mooney would yell in Tom's direction at the end of the lunch break.

"Hush up, you dumb Swiss," Tom would retort. Then, with a dramatic gesture, Tom would jab at Mooney with a sopping grease swab (used to apply grease to the machines). Occasionally Mooney accepted the challenge and to the delight of anyone who might be watching, the two would "fence" with the swabs. That was a fight to see! Neither man ever won, actually, as gobs of grease smacked into their hair, their ears and necks. For Tom, who kept his hair short, it wasn't much of a problem washing out the grease, but Mooney always needed Frieda to help him clean the grease out of his bushy hair. Frieda, meanwhile, was seldom

amused by such tomfoolery and she put an end to the battles
the day she told the Boss to go wash his own hair!

"You oughta clip that damn bush anyway," Tom often
teased Mooney, but to no avail. Mooney Warther was proud
of his hair.

"Mind your own business, you old corruptible bastard."
That was Mooney's favorite reply to Tom Moore. The fun
ended, of course, once the lunch break was over. Mooney's
job required total concentration and he and Tom did not mix
their pleasure with their toil.

While Mooney was not particularly fond of his job at the
American Sheet and Tin Plate Company (after all, his talent
was being wasted there), he obviously spent considerable
time thinking about the mill and its methods of production.
He found ways to make the mill more efficient and the jobs
less demanding. The shearmen wore heavy, leather aprons
to protect their clothes and their bodies from the sharp edges
of the iron but the aprons frequently wore out. Mooney
fashioned a flat, light-weight chain that hung over the
aprons and protected the leather. Thereafter, the aprons not
only wore longer but the chain took some of the strain off the
shearmen's stomach muscles.

Most of the shearmen found it difficult to push the heavy
sheets of steel through their shears. But after Mooney
invented a method for setting coasters into the shearmen's
tables, the shearmen rolled the sheets with ease, thus saving
energy and production time. This latter process was
eventually adapted by United States Steel.

Shearmen weren't the only employees to benefit from
Mooney's brilliance. The openers were forever wearing out
their work shoes until Mooney came to their aid. They used
the toes of their shoes to help them separate the sheets of iron
from the stacks and naturally that put holes in their shoes.
Mooney invented a steel cup that fit comfortably but snugly
over the tips of the workmen's shoes and thereafter the

openers could perform their jobs much faster and they were spared the expense of constantly replacing shoes.

Mooney's inventions promoted safety in the mill and also saved the mill thousands of dollars through increased production. Mooney was not remunerated for his ingenuity but, of course, he never asked for any compensation. He was simply pleased to make life easier for himself and his co-workers, and his satisfaction came from seeing his developments effectively employed.

For his thoughtfulness and cleverness and, of course, for his wit, the millmen appreciated Mooney Warther. Tom Moore may have referred to him as that "Dumb Swiss" to his face, but behind his back he was saying that Mooney Warther had "a head full of brains." Many of the millmen acclaimed Mooney's genious and marveled at his stamina. "He had to be very precise working with those engines. It was tedious work, difficult work, both his engines and the mill. I'll never know how he managed for so many years. Not one in ten million men could do it again," Tom said after Mooney's death in 1973.

Of course, not *all* millmen felt this way about Mooney Warther. Few men of genius have ever been accepted unwarily. There were men in the mill, as well as in Dover and Tuscarawas County, who were suspicious of Mooney and critical of his peculiar lifestyle and his occasional brusqueness. Some men detested Mooney simply because his parents were immigrants.

One winter morning at the mill Mooney observed several millmen sitting around the fireplace "chewin' the fat and wasting company time." Mooney could not tolerate loafers. Outside the plant, Mooney climbed a ladder to the roof of the building and carried with him a bucket of water. Cautiously he inched himself to the chimney stack and then he tossed the bucket of water down the flue. The splashing water spattered soot into the faces of the unsuspecting loafers and knocked several of them off their stools. The men knew that only Mooney Warther would do such a thing and a couple of them never forgave him for it. Mooney never saw any reason to apologize.

Some of the millmen were critical of Mooney's beliefs about God and they did not want to work next to him. Mooney was critical of organized religions and he was repulsed by the hypocrisy of once-a-week Christians. Some people interpreted this as atheistic and called Mooney an infidel. Mooney, however, believed that Christianity should be practiced consistently or not at all, and he never doubted the existence of a supreme power.

People also criticized Mooney for his political beliefs and his activism. He was considered unpatriotic when he traveled to nearby Canton to hear Socialist Party leader Eugene V. Debs who was campaigning for the Presidency. Debs was arguing for unemployment insurance, old age pensions and equal rights for women — patriotic concerns today but inflammatory in the early years of the twentieth century. When Debs was arrested for critizing the United State's involvement in World War I, Mooney was outraged. "Every man and woman is guaranteed the freedom to speak his mind." Apparently some of Mooney's fellow millmen did not agree with him as they denounced Debs and castigated Mooney behind his back. (Before Debs died in 1926 his citizenship had been revoked but fifty years after his death a United States Senate Committee voted to restore that citizenship and called Debs "a political activist ahead of his time.")

Mooney had learned early in life to ignore his critics and he never permitted the chatty millmen (or anyone else) to interfere with his work or his lifestyle. Nor could they alter his thinking. Living was too precious to Mooney Warther and unfavorable criticism could not dilute his convictions.

On the other hand, unfavorable criticism about Mooney

Warther was not widely expressed. In small-town Dover, people were not apt to forget that Mooney was the son of Muti Warther and the product of a respected and talented family. And Mooney himself had a reputation in and beyond Dover as an industrious, willing young man. People admired him for that. He was likely to succeed, most people thought.

Mooney's reputation, in fact, eventually led him out of the steel mill. Before he was twenty years old, Mooney was known as a keen cutler and he had a prosperous knife-making business. His kitchen knives were particularly in demand though his pocketknives were equally as popular. Knife-making was a hobby for Mooney, but it was a profitable hobby. At least once every year the mill was forced to close its doors in reaction to an unstable economy and then Mooney depended on his hobby to earn a living. Most millmen and their families suffered during these hard times, but Mooney always managed to get along.

The mill was down for several weeks before Christmas, 1922, and that year Mooney had one hundred six orders for pocketknives — fancy knives with gold coins set in their ivory handles that sold for a handsome price. Through the years Mooney had made thousands of these knives and they were recognized in many parts of Ohio. One afternoon a gentleman entered Mooney's workshop and pulled a coin-handled knife from his back pocket.

"You make this knife?" he asked the carver.

"Yep," Mooney said as he glanced at the knife and the stranger.

"Well, my name is Joe Hostetler and I'm an attorney in Cleveland," the man said as he extended his hand for Mooney to shake. Mooney was not impressed. "This knife was given to me by a friend and now I'd like you to use this whale tooth for the handle and set this three dollar gold piece in one side of the handle and this Roman coin in the other side. Will you do it?"

"Nope," Mooney said, continuing his work. "The mill's goin' back tomorrow and I won't have time for makin' knives. Got too much carvin' to do." (While the mill was down Mooney gave up carving so that he could devote full time to his knife business.)

"Carving?" asked Hostetler. "What carving?"

"Locomotives," said Mooney, inflecting some interest in his voice. "Come on and I'll show you. I keep 'em in the house."

When Joe Hostetler entered Mooney Warther's living room he stood in awe for a moment and stared at the dozen miniature locomotives on the mantel and on tables in the dimly lit room.

"These are magnificent," he said as Mooney allowed him to examine several of the engines. "Have these ever been written up in a newspaper?"

"Naaa," said Mooney. "I'm going to do several more before the project's finished — then I'll show 'em to the public."

"Well I hope you won't mind if I tell some of my friends in Cleveland about you and these carvings. These should be in the papers," Hostetler insisted.

Joe Hostetler's visit to Karl Avenue was to mean more to Mooney than the sale of another pocketknife — which he made before he returned to the mill — but Mooney wouldn't realize it until 1923. That summer, as Mooney neared thirty-eight years of age, he would leave the American Sheet and Tin Plate Company, somewhat hesitantly, even regretfully, but nonetheless fortunately. The Depression would close the American Sheet and Tin Plate Company for a final time in the early months of 1930. Men like Tom Moore, Jr. would lose years of seniority and a pension. For most millmen, the American Sheet and Tin Plate Company would become a nightmare — a nightmare from which some of them would never recover. But for Mooney Warther the American Sheet and Tin Plate Company was etched in his mind quite differently. He did not wish to forget it. For nearly a quarter of a century the mill was Mooney's livelihood. And it was good to him. The work was taxing and uninspiring, but it provided for his family. Mooney Warther cherished his memories of the steel mill, even after 1930, and to preserve his memories he eventually re-created the mill and the millmen in walnut and ivory. It was an appropriate gesture by the mill's most famous millman.

Chapter Five

The New York Central

Mooney Warther might have remained a local personality had it not been for the events of one bitter March night in 1923. It was a Saturday. Several executives of the New York Central Railroad were holed up for several days in a conference room of a Cleveland hotel. Pressure was on the New York Central to publicize the railroads in America and to encourage the public and industry to make better use of the system. The executives were carrying the brunt of the promotional campaign initiated by President Warren G. Harding. Early in his short tenure the President had stated that it would benefit the country if the railroads were better employed. A. H. Smith, then president of the New York Central Railroad, concurred with the President and decided to launch an encompassing campaign with the support of various organizations, including the National Grange and the American Farm Bureau Federation. In announcing the preliminaries for the campaign, Smith said the New York Central would create a demonstration train that would provide a variety of exhibits of mutual interest to the railroad and the country.

This demonstration train, eventually dubbed the Service Progress Special, was to be built in Cleveland's Collinwood Yards — thus the executives were meeting in that city. The men had finalized the exhibits, including a car devoted to industry and one to agriculture, and they were reasonably pleased with their progress. However, their major obstacle was promotion itself. How could they attract people into the Service Progress Special as it toured the Midwest?

The meeting was at a standstill in the pre-dawn hours of Sunday. One of the men, tired of talking and nauseated from the cigar smoke, said he was going out for fresh air and coffee and several of the men decided to join him. Before leaving the lobby of the hotel, one of the men bought a copy of the Sunday *Plain Dealer* and the rotogravure section fell to the floor. As he bent over to pick up the supplement, the executive noticed a photograph of a wavy haired man displaying a miniature locomotive. Excitement rushed through the executive's body as he turned the pages to the accompanying story about Mooney Warther.

"This is it . . . we've got it!" he yelled and ran to catch the other executives who were waiting for him outside the hotel. When he showed his cohorts the photographs and story about Mooney, they returned to the conference room, charged with enthusiasm about the possibility of getting Mooney Warther to join the Service Progress Special.

Early the next week, several of the executives traveled to Dover in search of Mooney. They found him at home carving and they asked to see his collection of locomotives. At first, Mooney did not realize the importance of the visit. He was constantly being interrupted by people who had heard of his carvings and wanted to see them, so he nonchalantly led the gentlemen to his living room, flipped the switch that set several of his miniature models in motion and watched the men in their disbelief. Finally, one of the men identified himself as Allen Rogers, a representative of the New York Central Railroad. He told Mooney that he wanted to make him a wealthy man.

Rogers outlined the plans for the Service Progress Special and showed Mooney how he and his carvings would complement the train. Mooney's curiosity was excited, of course, but his emotions were mixed. The New York

executive talked too fast for small-town Mooney and Mooney
hesitated when Rogers plopped a contract on the dining
room table and asked him to sign it.

"If you sign this contract," Rogers said persuadingly,
"you'll never work another day in a steel mill."

Mooney didn't believe that, but he contemplated the offer.
Certainly he'd like to escape the mindlessness and cruelty of
the mill, but then traveling with the New York Central would
take him away from his family, home and carving. That
would make him uncomfortable. On the other hand, the
Service Progress Special would be on the road for only five
months and his family would have the opportunity to visit
him whenever they desired. The money would be twice his
income from the mill and for considerably less time. Money,
however, was not a lure for Mooney. The lure of the New
York Central contract was unwritten but understood — it
would give Mooney the freedom he needed to carve and
complete the Evolution of the Steam Engine. Undoubtedly
that was the primary reason for Mooney's signing the
contract. It was an intriguing twist of events.

Of course, Frieda supported Mooney in this venture as she
was convinced the Boss needed to be out of the mill and free
to produce the Evolution of the Steam Engine. She was not
concerned about Mooney's being away from home — Frieda
Richard was a seasoned woman long before she had met
Mooney Warther and she could handle matters at home.

By modern standards the terms of Mooney's contract were
not excessive but in 1923 it was big money. From June, 1923
through spring, 1926, Mooney promised his time to the New
York Central Railroad for $5,000 a year. The first five
months he would be on the road with the Service Progress
Special and for the remainder of the contracted time,
Mooney's collection of locomotives would be displayed in
New York's Grand Central Station where Mooney agreed to
appear every month for several days of promotion. The

terms of the contract were sufficiently confining for the
railroad's purposes — the New York Central via the Service
Progress Special and Mooney Warther, would have a
spectacular promotion — and Mooney was satisfied with the
flexibility of the contract, the income, and the security that
the contract provided him for the next several years.

The signing of the New York Central contract was not
celebrated in any lavish manner in the Warther household.

The family, naturally, was excited and realized the
significance of the event, but it was business as usual.
Mooney signed the contract on March 31. Early that day he
completed a pocketknife and gave it to his oldest child, Tom.
That afternoon, just after signing the contract, he went to
work at the steel mill. While many men would have quit the
mill immediately upon signing such an agreement, or at
least soon thereafter, Mooney stayed on until a day or two
before the Service Progress Special was ready to roll. And
even then Mooney said only temporary goodbyes to his
fellow millmen; he expected eventually to return to the mill.

Mooney's contract stipulated that he provide fifteen
models for the Service Progress Special to be housed in a
specially-constructed Pullman car insured for $96,000. The
models, which had required nearly nine thousand hours of
carving time in the previous ten years of Mooney's life, were:
Sir Isaac Newton's Proposed Steam Locomotive, Murdock's
Road Locomotive, Reed's Steam Engine, George
Stephenson's Rocket, Trevithick's Locomotive, DeWitt
Clinton, Pioneer, Commodore Vanderbilt, B&O 100, 999
Empire State Express, Pacific Type, Columbia Type,
Dragon of 1848, the General and the Big Four. The Pullman
was stripped inside and redecorated to accommodate the
locomotives which were simply displayed along one side of
the car in an arrangement formulated by Mooney. The
carver left room for himself to walk behind the models to

point out their highlights and explain their histories to visitors.

On June 17, 1923, Mooney held his model of the Pacific Type and posed for newspaper photographers along side the Service Progress Special in Collinwood Yards. Then, he entered his personal Pullman — "I felt like a pig in a drugstore" — and the Service Progress Special pulled out of Cleveland. Originally, the New York Central executives had wanted Mooney to wear a tuxedo for his public appearances during the tour, but when Mooney tried on "the monkey suit," he felt uncomfortable and the railroad executives thought he looked even worse. A tuxedo was not Mooney's style and thereafter he dressed in business suits and street clothes. Mooney wasn't prepared for the attention showered on him by the New York Central people. He never did get accustomed to it but he was forever amused by it.

"They thought I was somebody," Mooney often mused in later years, "and I still don't believe I am."

During those five months on the road, the Service Progress Special traveled more than thirteen thousand miles on New York Central lines in Illinois, Michigan, Indiana, Ohio, Pennyslvania and New York and it was visited by nearly seven hundred eighty thousand persons. In practically every city where the special train stopped, newspapers headlined Mooney Warther and his collection of locomotives as the highlights of the exhibits. In city after city, for a morning or an afternoon, school children and adults filtered through the free exhibitions of the Service Progress Special. They left with a better appreciation of the railroad and enthusiasm for the system but they always left talking about that man "with the wild hair and the loud voice." Without a doubt Mooney Warther gave the railroads the kind of publicity that President Harding and A. H. Smith had intended. In return, the New York Central gave Mooney Warther fame, wealth and freedom to carve, but it also gave him countless anecdotes with which he would entertain audiences for the remainder of his life. Some of the best anecdotes of the Service Progress Special were captured in 1951 in *The Little Boy Who Found A Knife* by Caroline J. Pardee. She told the famous story of the day that Henry Ford wanted to meet the wood carver. She wrote:

> The train was scheduled for a whole day in Detroit to permit the school children to view the exhibits. It pulled in early, and Mooney and Frieda (Frieda occasionally joined Mooney) forgetting the change in time, couldn't rouse the waiters on the diner. They decided to see a bit of the city before the day's work began, and so went to Belle Isle, had breakfast, looked about, and returned to the train. But their unannounced absence caused great consternation among the New York Central officials, and they were urged henceforth to register their whereabouts. The time that Mooney had been AWOL had been selected by Henry Ford to visit the train to meet the Ohio carver. The officials were frantic, but Ford had left by the time Mooney returned. It was an expensive breakfast for the carver never did meet the great industrialist. He did, however, get wonderful service at meals thereafter!

After Ford's visit, he offered Mooney $75,000 for the collection of fifteen locomotives and $5,000 for the remainder of Mooney's life if he would move to Dearborn to live and carve. Mooney was gratified but his roots were in Dover and he had no desire to leave Karl Avenue. Besides, Mooney's style was to carve for himself and according to his own schedule. He could not accept the terms of Ford's offer.

In the early years of Mooney's career, he was known to give away his model locomotives. In 1917 he had given his

creation of the Sante Fe to W. C. Mills, then director of the
Ohio State Archaeological and Historical Society in
Columbus. Later, he gave the society duplicate models of the
General and the Big Four. So when the Service Progress
Special visited Columbus, the Ohio State Archaeological
and Historical Society placed the carvings that Mooney had
given them plus his Plier Tree (on loan to the society) on
special display. One evening, as author Pardee recalled the
event, Mooney went to view his models:

> He (Mooney) asked if the models would run. "Of
> course," the guard replied, "but do you think I'd
> run them just for you?" Then the loquacious
> caretaker discovered that his visitor was from
> Dover, where the carver Warther lived. He plied
> Mooney with questions about the carver and
> regaled him with bits of knowledge he himself had
> picked up. He wondered if Mooney knew him, had
> he ever been allowed in the carver's shop, and was
> Dover proud of him. Finally he asked, "Well, how
> do you people get along with a fellow who's so
> wound up all the time?" And his visitor responded,
> "Oh, we just let him run."

It wasn't often that Mooney went unrecognized. Usually it
was he who had difficulty remembering faces, including the
faces of his own family. On one occasion Mooney didn't even
recognize his wife!

The Service Progress Special had stopped in Youngstown,
Ohio one Sunday afternoon and Frieda joined some friends
who planned to visit Mooney and the train.

"Come on in and take a look, lady, it won't cost you a
dime," Mooney unknowingly coaxed Frieda as she
approached the Pullman.

"Is that so, Boss?" Frieda quipped.

"Well, Frieda," Mooney covered for himself, "I didn't even recognize you in that pretty new hat."

Mooney faced several crowds of strangers every day on the Service Progress Special and he used every bit of his personality to win their approval. His booming voice and his curly, uncontrollable hair were naturally part of the show — a very important part, in fact, at least to the New York Central executives. The executives panicked one afternoon when they heard that Mooney had left the train for a haircut. What a tragedy it would be if the showman returned with every hair slicked in place. The executives didn't relax until they spotted Mooney coming down the street, his blonde, wavy hair piled high and wind-blown. It was a comforting sight. He had only gone for a "shave and a trim."

Mooney's baritone voice was equally sacred to the railroad executives. A radio announcer, after interviewing Mooney for the first time, said, quite seriously, "We wouldn't have needed a mike with you, Mooney. We could have just opened the windows." Mooney's voice was an attraction itself and the railroad executives often worried that he might lose it. They were always pleased when someone asked Mooney not to talk so often or so loud. They snickered one night in a hotel lobby when they overheard the manager order a porter to "go tell that loud mouth on the fourth floor to shut up." Mooney was at a party and his penetrating voice was audible, and disturbing, in the lobby. The executives preferred that Mooney save his voice for the Service Progress Special.

The Service Progress Special treated Mooney Warther to a world whose existence he'd only previously read or heard about. He quickly grew lonely on the road — he missed his children and Frieda and his carving — but he absorbed every breath of this new life and met its challenges with enthusiasm. Like most good entertainers, Mooney played for his audiences and, fortunately, he matured mentally and emotionally with every audience, city after city. Mooney Warther was forever in touch with himself.

At the end of five months, in early November, 1923, the Service Progress Special ended its successful tour when it was pulled into New York City by the historic 999 Empire State Express. In 1893 the 999 was the world's fastest train when it pulled four baggage cars and three coaches at a speed of one hundred twelve-and-a-half miles per hour. (The record speed was not topped until 1926 when the Atlantic hit one hundred twenty-seven miles per hour in Ohio.) The 999 was retired upon pulling the Service Progress Special into Grand Central Station.

Following the rail tour Mooney was an honored guest at a banquet in New York City where the railroad executives attempted to lure him into more traveling with more money. Mooney stood to respond to the offer. "I'm highly honored," he said, "but my roof don't leak and I ain't hungry. I'm goin' home."

Mooney's collection of models, as contracted, remained in Grand Central Station through 1926 during which time it was viewed by three million persons from all parts of the globe. Once a month Mooney returned to New York City to appear with his collection but he never stayed for more than two or three days. It wasn't that he didn't enjoy the big city — he was overwhelmed by it — but he much preferred his small-town life in Dover, where, at last, he had the freedom to carve.

Chapter Six

Kinship

More than anything, including wealth and fame, Mooney Warther valued the lifestyle the New York Central Railroad afforded him. Like the artist who dreams of making a living by painting, Mooney Warther dreamed of making his living by carving. He didn't dream much, though, as even then dreams too often remained dreams. In actuality, Mooney and his family had always been accustomed to an artist's lifestyle. Now, though, for a few years at least, it would be a lifestyle of quality and quantity, of production and wealth. There was no longer a steel mill to interfere with the hours he spent in his workshop; there were no knives that *had* to be made for the family's welfare. Mooney's time was Mooney's time.

When he returned to Dover at the end of his stint with the New York Central, Mooney was eager to resume full time carving but first he wanted to re-acquaint himself with his family and friends. Of course, they couldn't wait to hear the stories of Dover's lively new celebrity and they had missed Mooney's philosophical attitude and his carefree spirit. Even before the New York Central trip, 331 Karl Avenue had often been a "meeting of the minds" on many Friday nights. Mooney and Frieda's relatives and friends customarily gathered there to discuss the events of their times in Dover and the nation, and, occasionally, the world. There was no television then and even radio was a luxury so they depended on conversation for their entertainment. In the spring or summer, the evenings were spent sitting on the wooden benches of the grape arbor that Mooney had built adjacent to Frieda's blossoming flower beds. The conversation was fortified with cheese and mixed nuts and a mug of homebrew, usually made by Mooney.

In November, 1923, however, when Mooney returned from New York, it was chilly and appropriate for Frieda's cozy living room warmed by a crackling fire. On his first Friday home, Mooney was surrounded by his wife and their four children: Tom, twelve; Florence, seven; Alice, five; and Wilma, three (David would be born in 1926). Throughout that evening they were visited by their families and neighbors who had heard that Mooney was back in Tuscarawas County. One of the proudest visitors that night was Muti Warther, then seventy-three.

That evening Mooney reminisced about his previous five months and as soon as several new faces appeared in the living room he'd tell the same stories again, re-living each moment as if it had just occurred the day before. There were so many visitors that night and so much to tell, that Mooney ran out of wood for the fireplace. Rather than send everyone home, or go out and chop more wood, he reached for his original model of the steel mill, which he had crudely carved in 1912, and tossed it upon the hearth. "Wasn't good enough anyway," Mooney told the startled crowd as he tossed the wooden caricatures of Tom Moore, Jr. and other millmen into the fireplace. One of Mooney's nephews, Walter Richard, salvaged the motor of the model and Mooney told him, "If I'd known you wanted the entire thing, I'da given it to ya for a load of wood."

These gatherings with friends and relatives were precious to Mooney and they continued through the years. Of course, the events would have occurred regardless of Mooney's lifestyle, but now they were all the more enriched with Mooney's fame.

Little changed in the Warther household after Mooney returned from the New York Central, but there was an adjustment period. It had been many years since Mooney could remember waking in the mornings and not dressing for the mill, and before that, the pasture land. Even Frieda, who now was kept busy by her youngsters, found it strange not packing a bucket for Mooney to carry to work. The children adjusted easily enough, but even they found it unusual to have their Pop at home twenty-four hours a day, most days.

Now that Mooney's children had grown older and he was living a more carefree life, the family spent more time together. In the winter, Mooney took the children sled riding on Red Hill and helped them build snow forts in the Calico Ditch. In the summers, they raced to the swimming hole, Frieda included, and they spent many afternoons at the "ideal spot," the name Mooney gave to their favorite place for picnics. To reach the "ideal spot" the Warthers climbed into their square-nosed boat and rowed across Sugar Creek. There they lunched on fried chicken and Swiss cheese and fresh fruits and vegetables from Frieda's garden. For dessert, there was usually Mooney's favorite: chocolate pie. After lunch, Mooney and his family explored the hillside and surrounding woods and Mooney talked about nature and life and the old days when he was a kid. Invariably, the walk led to that 1903 landmark where Mooney had once ended a farmer's chase.

Later, the family gathered around Frieda and she read aloud as Mooney and the children relaxed and listened. Mooney could read well for himself, as could the older children, but Mooney always said he absorbed more of it when he listened to Frieda. Usually she read Dickens and Crane, history books and encyclopedias, Bernarr McFadden's essays about health and, often, a biography of Lincoln.

Mooney had an uncanny knack for selecting rainy days for picnics. In the early part of the day, enroute to the "ideal spot," the weather would be warm, the sky bright and cloudless. But during the return home the Warthers were often caught in a cloud burst or by a threatening storm. After it had rained it was impossible to keep dry walking through the tall, clinging weeds of the bottom land between Sugar Creek and the Warther home. Once when they were thoroughly soaked, Mooney ran to their back yard and danced under a leaky spout while the rain gushed over his bushy hair. Frieda, the children, and Martha Hollinger (Frieda's sister who was along that day) were amused by Mooney's behavior but not surprised. By now, every member of the Warther family had learned to expect such antics.

At least one trip to the "ideal spot" was not at all humorous. A violent storm caught the Warthers just as they were climbing into their boat to cross Sugar Creek for home. Mooney pulled the boat onto the bank, turned it over and huddled his family underneath for safety. Fortunately the children were frightened by the thunder and lightning and they cried until Mooney and Frieda hurried them to the home of a nearby friend. After the storm they returned to the boat — or what was left of it. The boat had been crushed by a huge, fallen tree limb and had they remained under it they would have been seriously injured, if not killed.

The next week Mooney helped Tom and his friends build another boat and thereafter the Warther family returned many times to the "ideal spot."

Family unity was not uncommon to the Warther children but there was so much more time for it now. Even while Mooney worked in his shop, he often allowed the children to sit on his shop bench and watch his skilled hands. One year he made jewelry boxes for each of his girls and perhaps he showed his favoritism when he lined the jewelry box for

*AMERICAN SHEET AND TIN PLATE COMPANY. April, 1916.
Mooney, with chain over apron, stands in front of an unidentified
scrap bundler. Johnny Richard is between Mooney and Tom
Moore, Jr.*

Mooney and an early model.

WATERMELON FEAST. At Muti Warther's on Fifth St. circa
1908. Chuck Rufner is on the ground. On the bench from left is Fred
Warther, Mooney, Jake Warther and Herb Weber.

FRONTIER FAMILY. Mooney discovered this cabin in the woods
near Red Hill. Here, Frieda holds Florence while Mooney, back
from the hunt, looks on with young Tom.

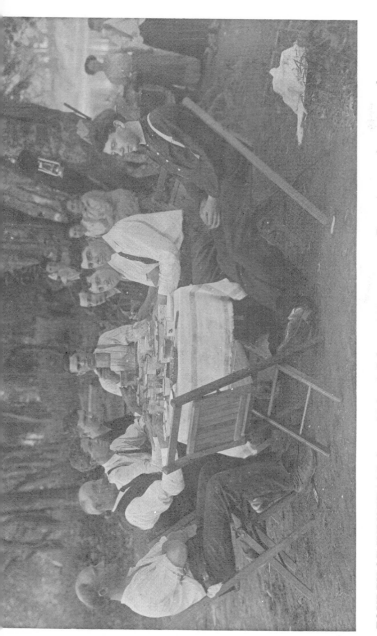

FOURTH OF JULY FEAST. Second Island, July 4, 1910, enroute to Zoar. As was the custom, the men sat for dinner while the women cooked and served. Mooney, in white shirt and tie with suspenders, is third from the left. Fred Warther, with feet crossed, is in the foreground and next to him is brother Jake. Second Island was in the Tuscarawas River.

RELAXING. *From left is Ike Trubey; Mooney; Tom Warther, Mooney's oldest son; and Christian Richard, Frieda's brother.*

DETERMINATION. *Shy Fred and showman Mooney with their truck, circa 1927.*

AT WORK on the General, famous Civil War locomotive.

THE EVOLUTION OF THE STEAM ENGINE. On display.

MOONEY AND FRIEDA. On the back porch at 331 Karl Avenue.

FRIEDA'S BUTTONS. The display includes a button from a dress worn by the wife of Abraham Lincoln.

HENRY MORGAN challenges the famous carver to a game of chess with the set that Mooney made especially for the TV-personality.

THE BUST. Presented to Mooney in Crater Stadium, June 16, 1963.

Florence, his eldest daughter, with redwood. The others were in plain walnut.

As the children grew older they each spent time alone with their father, usually on long walks at midnight or in the pre-dawn hours to Red Hill and out to the village of Sugarcreek. During those walks Mooney philosophized about life and values and family and generally coached his children through their adolescent years. These walks provided the Warther children a unique insight into a man who was rapidly becoming a public figure and who might otherwise not ever have had a private moment to spend with them in their formative years.

Another benefit of the New York Central, which contributed to family togetherness, was money. There was more of it now than Mooney had ever dreamed likely. Most of it was wisely saved but Mooney splurged in 1926 when he bought a Model-T four door sedan. In 1909 Mooney had owned one of the first automobiles in Dover, a 1907 Olds, but he scrapped it shortly after his marriage in 1910 and hadn't replaced it. One of Mooney's shortcomings was that he could not drive. He was coordinated enough and he knew how to operate an automobile but he couldn't keep it on the road and he had little sense about speed.

Hezzy was the name Mooney gave to his Model-T but only the unwise ever saw the inside of Hezzy with Mooney behind the wheel. Once someone discovered his erratic, unsafe driving manners, Mooney lost another rider. Hezzy couldn't be taken out alone, however, as Mooney always needed help pushing the automobile up hills. Usually he could convince his nieces and nephews to ride with him; they didn't mind the speed and they were amused by Mooney's habits of driving on sidewalks and into ditches.

Fortunately no one was ever seriously injured in any of Mooney's accidents, although more than one unknowing rider was stunned when his head cracked against the bare, steel roof of Hezzy as Mooney bounced the machine over bumps and curbs. Mooney's most serious accident occurred one Sunday in the late 1920s after he enticed Frieda and the children into an afternoon drive. Mooney drove Hezzy to the country and out one of the dirt roads where years before he had grazed the cows. There he explained to the children how he and their Uncles Fred and Jake used to catch black snakes in the hills and hang them from tree limbs. As the children cocked their heads to examine every tree that their father pointed out, trees that undoubtedly the children had seen time and time before, Mooney became more engrossed in his story and less aware of the road. Just as he pointed to a cow grazing on the green hillside, Hezzy barreled over a steep embankment and rolled into Sugar Creek. Mooney helped Frieda and the children to dry ground and then he sprawled on the creek bank and roared with laughter. Frieda, this time, was not amused by the Boss and while walking back to town she convinced Mooney that, indeed, he could not drive an automobile. Jake helped Mooney tow Hezzy home and there they jacked up the automobile and set it on blocks. Hezzy remained immobile through the Depression and until 1940 when Tom took it over. Mooney, after this accident with his family, never sat behind the wheel of another automobile. Thereafter, when walking didn't suit him, he rode a bicycle which he dubbed his Cadillac.

Most of the pleasures of the Warther family didn't come from money or money objects, so jacking up Hezzy was no sacrifice. Fishing, camping, walking, talking, picnicking and working together gave the Warthers more enjoyment than a country ride — besides, there was less risk.

The Warther kinship, of course, was extended to the neighborhood gang of the time, which after the mid-1920s consisted mostly of Tom's friends. Mooney, however, was still the feature attraction. He spent more time with this gang than any of those that preceded or followed, and, sadly, it was the last real gang. Perhaps that's why it's so well remembered. The gangs that followed were victims of the Depression, the wars and the changing social scene and they could never experience all the benefits of an ideal Warther gang. In the mid-1930s, for example, a land-hungry Godfrey Smith came along and changed the course of Sugar Creek, making the water shallow and muddy. As a result, The Elm was destroyed and swimming in the creek was no longer desirable or feasible.

But in the mid-1920s the gang was supreme. It included Kenny Espenschied, whom Mooney later presented with one of his locomotives. Kenny became one of Dover's leading restauranteurs and for many years operated Espenschied's, known for tasty steak dinners and fresh seafood. There was also Johnny Meese, Mooney's nephew, who lived next door to him and would eventually work for Mooney during the war years when Mooney's knives were in great demand. Other nephews who were in the gang included Bob Meese, Jim Warther and Don Warther, Jake's son, who inherited his father's repair shop in Dover and ran it successfully for many years. Chester Kennedy, a neighbor, was another member of that famous gang.

Mooney made each of the gang members a hunky knife, named in honor of the Hungarian who had designed the knife for Mooney. It was a large pocketknife connected to a short chain and each knife was numbered and had Mooney's name cut into the handle. The youngsters hooked the chains to their fashionable bib overalls and displayed them proudly as a hunky knife was the mark of a Warther gang member.

Kenny Espenschied and Tom, Mooney's son, were together most days during the mid-1920s. They walked to and from school and played afterwards in the Calico Ditch and they often "slept over" in each other's homes. As a result, they spent more time with Mooney than any of the other gang members. Usually they helped Mooney in the shop, keeping the fire burning and handing him tools; grinding knife blades and, undoubtedly, getting in the way. Often Mooney took time to show the pair how to use his knives and tools. Once he taught them how to carve bone into the shape of an arrowhead — the trick was filing the bone flat and then using a rattail file to shape it. Kenny also learned to carve the tiny, wooden pliers that had become Mooney's trademark and one of his proudest moments was the day he ran to his home on Tuscarawas Avenue to show his parents the pliers that Mooney had helped him cut in white pine.

Mooney made bows and arrows for Tom and Kenny and they went hunting out Winfield Road one afternoon. They stumbled onto a farm that was owned by one of Kenny's uncles and there in the barnyard they spotted a large, brown rooster. Perhaps if the bird hadn't been so insistent on flapping about the yard, the boys wouldn't have been so tempted by it. They hesitated, but the rooster was a challenge for their bows and arrows. Taking aim, they fired on the count of three, and by some eerie fortune Tom's arrow crossed Kenny's and pinned the rooster's head to the side of the barn. The boys couldn't believe it themselves and they knew that without the rooster Mooney would never believe their story. So they took the rooster home and had Mooney snap their photo in front of the cave in the Calico Ditch, all the while holding the live rooster upside down by its claws. Then, they killed the rooster, dressed it and cooked the fowl over an open fire. It was a meal they would never forget.

The next day Kenny's uncle appeared at Mooney's and handed the boys a bill for two dollars. Either someone had tipped him off about the rooster's disappearance, or, as he claimed, he had watched the boys the day before from a window in his farmhouse. At any rate, he verified their story and Kenny and Tom worked for Mooney for several days to earn the money to pay their debt.

As Mooney spent time with Tom and Kenny, he grew to appreciate Tom's young friend. In fact, Kenny and Mooney developed a close relationship that lasted until Mooney's death. In 1957 Mooney carved, for no obvious reason, a pair of pliers with Kenny's name cut into it and he mailed the pliers to Kenny at the restaurant. When the postmaster spotted the Warther pliers at the post office, he recognized the value and delivered the pliers in person to Kenny.

A few years later, and again for no obvious reason, Mooney called Kenny to his museum on Karl Avenue and gave him a model of the Commodore Vanderbilt. It was one of the last models that Mooney gave away. Soon after presenting Kenny with the carving, Mooney mailed him a letter to explain the gift:

Feb. 12, 1962

To my friend Kenny Espenschied. Just a few words to tell you just why I gave to you that hand carved model of a locomotive.

You have always impressed me. Ever since you were a boy playing in my play grounds as many other children did.

You never quarreled, you always knew your place and in that same spirit you grew up.

I watched you go up the ladder of success rung by rung. You are an inspiration to me and many others — Many are they who played there then and now come back and bring their children to show them that same old play grounds—Specially the big swing and the cave you knew so well.

Now Kenneth if you get as much pleasure out of that model as I did making it and giving it to you, then we are both happy.

Sincerely yours
(Signed) Ernest Mooney Warther

At the end of the letter, next to a stamp of Lincoln, Mooney wrote, "Like the man on this stamp, he never quarreled, he always knew his place." And below that he included this verse:

> I'm slow in writing this letter to you
> Now I'm past 76, it goes all the harder
> So to write this letter
> Twas no fun
> For the pen weighed a ton
> The paper lay under a key lost lock
> And the ink was solid rock.

Below the poem, Mooney signed his name a second time.

Mooney Warther saw the perfect gang member in Kenny Espenschied. Of all the children who had played in his back yard, he chose Kenny to honor. The model, along with the letter relating Kenny to Abraham Lincoln, was the greatest compliment that Mooney Warther could pay to any man. At the time of Mooney's gift, Kenny was nearing fifty years of age and he was exuberant. He immediately hired a carpenter to build a showcase for the Commodore Vanderbilt and for several weeks the model was displayed in his restaurant. Later, he moved the model to a display in his home.

When Kenny accepted Mooney's locomotive he recalled those old days when most any inquisitive youngster could win Mooney's favor. How good it was to have Mooney Warther listen to your problem, or solve your problem! Kenny hadn't felt so close to Mooney since the night in 1926 when Mooney carved the initials KE into the wooden bench outside his workshop. That was the second greatest Warther compliment. Mooney spent endless hours on that bench, carving and talking with family and friends and youngsters. On those nights you could sense the uniqueness of Mooney Warther. He seemed to know something about everything and yet he was never assuming. He was proud but never arrogant. He had a temper but it was offset by a sense of humor that let him laugh at himself more than at anyone else. His loudness, mixed with his unyielding hair and his country manners gave him a shocking roughness, but it was smoothed over by his effervescence and his personal warmth. None of this mattered, though, on those starry nights when Mooney's voice pierced the silence of nearby Sugar Creek and echoed in the Tuscarawas Valley. Those nights, what mattered most was that Mooney Warther was himself.

Chapter Seven

Golden Years of Carving

As much as Mooney enjoyed socializing, he never wasted a moment of time that should have been spent working. Next to his family and friends, Mooney had missed his carving while he was on the Service Progress Special. In the pre-morning hours immediately after his return home, Mooney could be found working in his shop, which by this time had been moved to the rear of his lot. A fireplace warmed the early morning chill and brightened the wooden bench where he continued to carve his now famous Evolution of the Steam Engine. The 999 Empire State Express, which Mooney had started carving during his tour, was now on the workbench. He had previously carved two models of the 999 but he gave away both of them. The exact starting date for this third model was not recorded, but Mooney was constantly interrupted while finishing it. There was always someone who wanted to visit him or a tourist who had heard about his carvings and wanted to see them or a chore around the house that needed his immediate attention. Of course, there were also his monthly trips to New York City where he was expected to spend several days promoting his collection in Grand Central Station.

Despite these delays, the 999 was completed on March 3, 1924 and the next day Mooney left for New York City where thousands of passersby, residents of New York and visitors to that thrill-packed city, streamed by the Warther collection every day in Grand Central Station and marveled at its magnificence. Prominent and lesser-known visitors stood for perhaps half an hour and examined the intricate models. When Mooney was in the station, of course, people were around him the entire day as he entertained them, answered their queries and acknowledged their compliments. Once, on December 4, 1923, Mooney met the celebrated carvers of Oberammergau. "I met the famous German carvers in the Grand Central Palace in New York City," Mooney wrote in his diary which he had resumed during his tour. "They admitted that the models were the finest thing they ever saw that was carved by hand."

Such vibrant moments in New York's Grand Central Station fired Mooney's ego, but nevertheless he didn't linger on those trips to New York City. His work was at home in Dover.

On March 17, 1924, Mooney began the Mother Hubbard, Columbia Type 694. He averaged six hours carving time through the remainder of March, according to his diary, and the rest of his time was devoted to chores and making bows and arrows, plus "four billiard balls" for the neighborhood gang.

Mooney continued to devote six to seven hours a day to his carving through late April, 1924, but then he wrote in his diary, "Spring has come, the garden is to be spaded and other work about the house, so the engine hours will be short for a while." "Short" to Mooney meant four hours daily, usually put in before dawn. Once he even worked on Sunday morning, which was against his principles. "Oh, I slip a little in on Sunday," he told his diary.

Come spring, neither Mooney's fame nor the Evolution of the Steam Engine stood in the way of responsibility. Mooney's mother and several of her elderly friends in Dover relied on Mooney and his brothers to spade their plots of ground every year so that they could plant vegetable gardens. The chore was a bit easier now that Mooney's son,

Tom, and many of Tom's cousins, could help out, but even so
it took the gang ten hours to spade and rake Muti's garden.
One hundred by two hundred feet was plenty of garden space
for one old Swiss woman but Muti didn't grow vegetables
just for herself — most of her produce she canned and gave
away. One spring Muti asked her boys to put a walk through
the center of her garden and so Mooney and his brothers
mixed a batch of cement and taught their youngsters to lay a
cement walk.

After Muti's garden was tilled the men would dig into
another garden at Jake's, or Mooney's, or at one of Muti's
friends. And at the end of every garden there was a picnic of
ham sandwiches, cheese, housenpepper and a four-hopper (a
keg of beer).

In 1924, in addition to spading gardens, Mooney also had
to catch up with chores that were left undone the summer
before at 331 Karl Avenue. In the middle of May he stripped
the house of its spouting and paint. He painted through late
May and completed the job with new spouting and eaves and
screens for every window. When he finished the house he
painted his workshop and also the windmill in his backyard.
Mooney had made the windmill from black walnut and
erected it in his mother's yard on his wedding day in 1910.
Then, when he and Frieda moved to Karl Avenue, the
windmill was also moved and it became a conversation
piece. "Whenever I paint the house," Mooney would tell
anyone who asked, "I paint the windmill and it makes me
feel young again. I want to see which runs longer, the
windmill or me. It's had to have some repairs through the
years, but then, so have I."

In early June, 1924, Mooney spent several days in New
York City but on the ninth he returned and resumed carving
the Mother Hubbard which was slowly nearing completion.
He averaged only three hours carving time per day in June,
as it was the month of the swimming hole and there was a

new crew of youngsters in the neighborhood who needed to learn to swim.

By July, though, Mooney was carving up to ten hours some days and on July 27, after spending three days in New York City, he finished the engine of the Mother Hubbard. On the next day he took six hours to begin the tender, the railroad car that followed the engine and carried coal and water to supply steam. He completed the tender on August 18. Then, Mooney packed his family's suitcases and headed for Niagara Falls — by train, of course. (One of the fringe benefits of the New York Central contract was that Mooney and his family could travel free by rail to any city in the United States.)

On August 22 the Warthers returned to Dover where Mooney found a telegram inviting him to join the New York Central on a special seven-week tour. Mooney returned to the train station and was gone through October 13.

On the fourteenth Mooney was back in his workshop and he told his diary, "I made a wrong mistake." It's not certain if he regretted the seven-week tour or if he erred in the carving of the Mother Hubbard. At any rate, on October 30, Mooney's thirty-ninth birthday, he carved for six hours and finished the Mother Hubbard after a total of seven hundred ninety-five carving hours. The model included four thousand four hundred twelve parts. "It's a great day for me," Mooney confided to his diary.

By the fall of 1924 Mooney could cope with the constant interruptions and he was able to complete one model after another. The First Passenger Mogul Locomotive, built by the Baltimore and Ohio Railroad for the 1876 Centennial exhibition, was begun on December 1, 1924 and completed the next May 7. The Illinois, first passenger engine to burn anthracite coal, was begun on June 10, 1925 and completed October 10, ". . . just as the sun went down and at the first fall of snow. Tom and his gang had a fire in the cave all day."

The Commodore Vanderbilt, which could run forty miles per hour in 1870, was begun on November 23, 1925 and completed March 10, 1926. That was Mooney's fortieth locomotive.

The General, the famous Civil War locomotive, later romanticized by Walt Disney, was begun on May 18, 1926 and completed the following November 18. Mooney carved four models of the popular General in his career: one was given to the Ohio Historical Museum in Columbus and the other three, including one entirely of ivory, are in the Warther Museum in Dover. When Mooney completed the 1926 model, he wrote, "She is a peach," a popular quip which he also used for attractive women.

Most of the models Mooney carved during this period were duplicates of models he had carved earlier in his career. The reason for the redundancy was the carver's enterprise. As early as 1920 Mooney was often requested to display his carvings at fairs and exhibitions. Being a showman, he was pleased to oblige. The fame that came with the Service Progress Special encouraged other such requests for Mooney's collection. Mooney reasoned, however, that if his locomotives were in Grand Central Station (where they would remain through the spring of 1926) he'd have no opportunity to display them in other sections of the country, particularly in Tuscarawas County where now practically every other resident wanted to gawk and fuss over the creations of their hometown boy. The only solution was for Mooney to carve duplicate models.

Mooney also realized that eventually his commitments to the New York Central Railroad would be exhausted — and vice versa. By the spring of 1926 Mooney would be without an income and after nearly three years of enjoying his artist's lifestyle, a comfortable artist's lifestyle, he had no intentions of returning to the mill. That would be a final resort.

The carver wanted to protect his freedom and at the same time ensure an income to support his family. He was eager, then, to meet C. A. Radford one summer day to discuss a showing at the St. Louis Industrial Exposition, set for two weeks in the fall of 1926. Radford, the publicity manager of the Big Four, was sent to Dover on a muggy June afternoon to convince Mooney to sign a contract to appear at the exposition. As eager as Mooney was, he was also intently busy the day Radford visited, and it appeared to Radford that the carver was not interested in his offer. That discouraged the Big Four's publicity agent, but even more frustrating were the pesty children who kept interrupting the meeting. Just when Radford thought he had Mooney's attention, some kid would pop his head in the workshop and shout, "Come on, Mooney, let's go swimming." Mooney would motion away the youngster and continue carving. Radford would begin another approach for the carver's attention but again, just as he sensed some interest, another kid would bound into the workshop. "Mooney, when are we goin' swimming?"

Convinced that he could not undermine the gang, Radford finally told Mooney to name any price and he'd agree to it. Mooney wanted a thousand dollars a week, plus expenses. The contract was signed. Months later, when the Big Four wanted Mooney and his collection to appear at Dixie Terminal in Cincinnati and then the Historical and Industrial Expositions in that same city, Radford advised the Big Four brass to "Send him (Mooney) a telegram, for God's sake, and tell him to keep those kids away!"

The public's response to these exhibitions and to the New York Central tour (which had covered six states, primarily in the Midwest) convinced Mooney that people throughout the country were eager to see his collection of carvings. So he decided to put his collection on the road himself and he invited his brother Fred to assist him.

Fred Warther, who was now called Fritzy, was a frustrated chief engineer in Dover's light plant in 1927. Before that, he had been a master mechanic (a trade he learned on his own) at Penn Mold in Dover. Before that he had worked in the mill. Mooney knew that his brother wanted less confining work, preferably work that involved travel, and Fritzy didn't hesitate a moment when Mooney revealed his plans and asked him to take the carvings "Coast to coast and border to border," stopping in the small towns of America so that the people could view the works of "the master carver," as Mooney was now billed.

The brothers purchased a large panel truck and renovated it to suit their needs. Special padding and insulation was installed inside the truck to protect the models from the perils of the road. The body of the truck was re-designed so that it would open into a display. And, to make the traveling more convenient and less costly, Mooney and Fritzy included two bunks in the back of the truck.

Fritzy, however, drove most of the miles alone, with Mooney joining him every so often in choice states for a week or three, but only when Mooney could break away from his work in Dover where he continued to carve the Evolution of the Steam Engine. The road show was important to Mooney's income, but it was not immediately crucial, and he tried not to overextend himself. The Evolution of the Steam Engine, far from being completed, was most important.

Three months after Mooney completed the General, in 1926, he had been carving the First American Type, built in 1844. Twelve weeks later, on May 10, 1927, he completed the locomotive. Later that month he began the Pioneer, the first locomotive to pull a train west of Chicago in 1836 and, after countless interruptions, he completed it on January 3, 1928.

In 1928 there were no interruptions for Mooney the carver. He completed six locomotives that year and started a seventh. As soon as he laid down his knife on January 3, he began another DeWitt Clinton and completed it March 6. During the nine weeks that he devoted to the DeWitt Clinton, Mooney also carved "three pocketknives, not less than thirty paring knives and butcher knives, besides a number of other things including the Lindbergh Cane." (The Lindbergh walking cane, only modestly referred to in his diary reveals another of Mooney Warther's talents. Three feet long and made of walnut, the cane is topped with a handle in the form of a parachute and below that a remarkable bust of Lindbergh. Mooney's sculpting was not a latent talent — he had displayed it earlier in the cane he had made in honor of Lincoln — but it was not often displayed. This talent, combined with his talent for carving, led many artists, psychologists and mathematicians to remark that Mooney was a genius. Of course, that didn't impress Mooney. Lindbergh impressed Mooney, and because of Lindbergh's transatlantic flight, Mooney believed he deserved to be so commemorated. The carving of the Lindbergh walking cane marked the only time in Mooney's career that he worked on two major carvings concurrently.)

The day Mooney completed the DeWitt Clinton, on March 6, 1928, he started George Stephenson's Rocket, the first high speed locomotive built in England in 1829. It had managed twenty-nine miles per hour! On May 10, Mooney started carving Trevithick's Locomotive, the first engine to run on rails, built in 1803 in South Wales. Top speed, five miles per hour! Trevithick was credited with inventing the first locomotive. Mooney completed the model on July 30, 1928.

Next, on August 1, he began Reed's Road Locomotive or Steam Carriage, built in 1791. The original locomotive, called the First Multitubular Boiler, operated only in forward gear, much to the dismay of the inventor. It wasn't discovered until mid-way through the carriage's trial run that the mechanism could not be reversed, and so it was

abandoned to rust. Mooney completed his model on
September 12.

Murdock's Locomotive of 1784, which had three wheels
and was impractical, was begun on September 28 and
Mooney carved it in just twelve days. On October 11 he
began carving Sir Isaac Newton's Proposed Locomotive of
1680. The Tea Kettle, as Isaac's locomotive was also called,
included six hundred seventy-four parts and Mooney
finished it on November 14.

The six models that Mooney completed in 1928 were
excellent practice for the model that he began on December
11 of that year. The New York Central's Hudson Type was
"the King of them all," according to Mooney. The engine
could pull twenty passenger coaches at one hundred miles
per hour! The model was to take one thousand three hundred
seventy hours to carve, spread over sixteen months, and
require seven thousand two hundred sixty parts. Beginning
with the Hudson Type, Mooney resumed a day-to-day
account in his diary which explained the significant events
of the day and recorded the number of hours he spent
carving that day. December 17 was "blue Monday" but he
carved for five hours; December 31 "mother is sick" and he
carved for four hours; January 17, "went to Richards for a
blow out" (party), and he carved five hours. Occasionally,
Mooney worked on Sundays, but only when necessary. "You
gotta carve bell ropes on Sunday," Mooney used to explain,
"as you can't make a bell rope without swearin' and you
can't swear on Sunday." Carving bell ropes required
meticulous concentration and Mooney was particular about
making them look authentic. Bell ropes were strung along
the front sides of steam locomotives and pulled by the
engineers to sound the engine's bell. Mooney carved the
ropes in ivory, a difficult task as the actual bell ropes, when
they were not taut, had a natural slack. And Mooney insisted
his ivory ropes reflect that slack. Ivory, however, does not

bend and so Mooney had to carve the slack into his finished bell ropes. To make the task even more difficult, but more realistic, Mooney filed the tiny ropes to give them a coarse texture. The ivory had a tendency to crack under the slightest pressure of the file, and when that happened Mooney had to begin anew. *Nothing* angered him more — and when Mooney carved bell ropes, everyone knew to stay clear of his shop — even if it were Sunday!

Mooney's fingers suffered from the minute details of his carvings and on many days he wrote in his diary "My finger tips are worn through." Still, he continued to carve, painful though it was.

Mooney's momentum would have carried him through the Hudson Type in less than sixteen months, but unfortunately, in late February of 1929, Frieda became suddenly very ill. Mooney explained the situation in his diary: "My wife was taken to the hospital and was in a serious condition so work stopped until the 25th when I got in one hour and as things look better so will work go better. Like a ship wrecked sailor sees shore and takes heart once more."

Shore was more than a month away, though, as in March Mooney was still visiting Frieda two and three times a day in the hospital. "The ship wrecked sailor is not yet dry. So the wife is still in the hospital."

Frieda had contracted Bright's disease (kidney infection) and she nearly died. The trauma of the illness took away her strength and soured her spirits. It was a dreadful time. She remained in the hospital through March 20 but even at home she was confined to bed for several additional weeks. In the meantime, Mooney put up his knife and tended to his children and home. He painted the house and worked the garden. After Frieda was brought home he devoted himself to her needs and yet he made time for other responsibilities. One afternoon he repaired Muti's chicken coop and on another day he and his brothers spaded their mother's garden.

While Mooney remained good natured through Frieda's illness, he missed carving, particularly the Hudson Type. By late June, when Frieda had regained her strength and was able to leave her bed, it was obvious that Mooney could soon return to his workshop. To celebrate the good news, as well as Frieda's recovery, Mooney went "on a little toot."

Soon thereafter Mooney took Florence and traveled to Collinwood Yards (perhaps by streetcar) to study the Hudson Type. Occasionally Mooney carved from blueprints and photographs but he preferred to examine the real thing when he had the opportunity. Often he'd ask his nephew, Walter Richard, to drive him to Cleveland or to the train yards in nearby Dennison where he could crawl around the engines and inspect every curve and line. Mooney insisted on including even the most incidental parts in his locomotives — regardless of whether or not they could be seen by the casual observer. The carver prided himself on accuracy and challenged anyone to find an error in any of his models. Only one man, and he was a B&O engineer, ever discovered an error in a Warther train. Vic Kuhn, whom Mooney called The Big Engineer, once informed the master carver that he had connected the wrong tender to one of the engines.

"My God," Mooney roared when Vic told him about it. "Thousands of people have looked at this train and never saw that." Mooney thanked Vic for the correction and changed the tender on the spot.

Despite his celebration and his impatience to return to carving in mid-1929, Mooney did little cutting that summer. The house and the garden, which Frieda was too weak to keep, occupied much of his time and what time he could spare he needed to make knives to earn his living. Medical bills were costly. On August 22 Mooney carved for an hour-

and-a-half — "getting started again," he wrote in his diary, but then it was early September before he carved again. Slowly Mooney regained his momentum and before September was through he was averaging four hours a day. He completed the engine of the Hudson Type on September 20, despite countless interruptions and then he ordered blueprints for the tender. On September 11 Mooney went to the dentist — "Wow," he wrote in his diary. On the 17th he went to a "corn cutting party," on the 18th "a funeral," and the 26th was "the day after the night before." That phrase, which meant that Mooney was hung-over, occurred occasionally throughout his diaries.

In early October Mooney wrote, "the blueprints (for the tender) not yet here so I'll take about two weeks with the truck." When he returned to Dover the blueprints were waiting for him and he averaged five to six hours of carving time a day through November. In December, however, he was interrupted with orders for fifty knives for Christmas gifts and he worked intently and filled the orders by the nineteenth. "Now I'm all set to start on the model again and give her hell."

Mooney began the new year with a fourteen-hour carving day on January 3 and he continued to work long hours as he was now anxious to complete the challenging Hudson Type. On March 11 he spent seven hours and carved ninety-one letters to inlay in the base of the locomotive. But through the remainder of the month, and most of April, he accomplished very little in his workshop. He made knives several days, carved wooden pliers other days, mounted arrowheads, went to Cleveland, and painted the kitchen — but he carved very little. Finally, near the end of April, he managed to ignore all interruptions and he carved for several hours a day. Then, on April 28, he laid the rails and set the Hudson Type upon them. "That finished the engine 5200 of the New York Central," he wrote. He noted that the materials cost him

$147.05. It was a proud day.

After the Hudson Type Mooney needed a less complicated encore and so he carved Peter Cooper's Tom Thumb, the first successfully built locomotive. The engine, however, had not been very efficient. It took an hour-and-a-half to travel thirteen miles! After the engine lost a race with a horse, its popularity fizzled. Mooney carved the engine between May 14 and October 24, 1930.

The next year, Mooney carved only one engine, the Mallet Articulated Triplex Compound, built for the Erie Railroad in 1913. The slender model, with 9,504 parts, carved in Belgian Congo ebony, required 1,358 carving hours between January 19 and September 27.

It was almost a year before Mooney carved another locomotive. Frieda's illness lingered and Mooney spent more time on the road and at exhibitions and festivals, trying to make his funds meet his expenses. He couldn't resist carving much longer, however, when on September 26, 1932 he initiated a challenge even greater than the Hudson Type. He started carving the Great Northern, the mountain type locomotive of 1930. For this rugged locomotive Mooney again used ebony from Africa. His model, heavily inlaid with mother of pearl on ebony, took 1,600 hours to carve and was completed on May 1, 1933. The Great Northern, Mooney's favorite carving, was the climax of his career. Ironically, the completion of the model brought an end to the lifestyle that the artist had enjoyed for so many years. Such a lifestyle was no longer feasible for Mooney Warther. America's prosperity was of an age gone by and of an age to come. Mooney's income from the New York Central Railroad, much of which had been saved, had now been spent. Frieda's illness was costly and what money her bills didn't take was absorbed by the Depression. Road exhibitions were now crucial to Mooney's welfare. The Golden Years of Carving had ended.

Chapter Eight

Nickel Museum

Mooney was right in thinking that the people of America would want to see his locomotives. Newspapers across the country had publicized him as the world's master carver during the Service Progress Special tour and the publicity continued, though not as heavily, while his models were in Grand Central Station. Mooney's name was not readily recognized in all parts of the country but people were always curious to hear about Mooney Warther, the carver, the knifemaker, the eccentric. They were even more eager to meet him. Consequently, Mooney's truckload of miniature models, Determination, was enthusiastically welcomed from California to Massachusetts and from the Dakotas to Texas and all points between. Droves of interested Americans, children and adults, anticipated the annual arrival of the Warther truck with the intricate carvings. Each year they hoped that this round, the carver himself would come along. From the late 1920s through the mid-twentieth century, Determination was a cherished cultural experience for the small towns of America. And, especially during the Depression, the admission price was popular — it was free. Mooney and Fritzy were shrewd businessmen who wanted to avoid the cumbersome tax papers that were incidental to an admission charge. As a result, they invited their visitors to contribute to a donation box, which was continuously baited with coins.

Mooney was also right about asking Fritzy to run this

endeavor for him. "Now I'm free as a bird," Fritzy told his brother after they agreed on the road tour. "This is my kind of job." Fritzy loved traveling and experiencing various parts of the country and there seemed to be no end to it for him. Even in 1977, when he turned 95 years old, Fritzy was still traveling and by that time he had seen *every* part of the country, most of it at least a dozen times.

Mooney's brother was perhaps the most philosophical of the Warther boys, more so even than Mooney, who was three years' Fritzy's junior. Because Fritzy was an introvert his ideas were not often expressed outside his home, or his truck, and it was necessary to know him intimately to understand him and to appreciate his wit. He was a character worth studying and admiring.

One philosophy which underscored Fritzy's life was this: Have the time to make something, the time to sell it and finally the time to spend it. In the late 1920s, Mooney found the time to make it, Fritzy the time to sell it, and both of them found time to spend it, though with two growing families to feed and cloth, there wasn't *much* to spend after the necessities.

In the beginning, to adjust to this new lifestyle which would keep him from his wife and daughters for long periods of time, Fritzy toured towns in Ohio and showed Mooney's collection at fairs and homecomings. "I'd go into a town and stop at the police station to ask the chief or the mayor for permission to set up a show on the square or on one of the downtown streets. Free of charge to the public, of course — no one ever turned me down," Fritzy boasted in later years. Fritzy remained in town for a day, maybe two "as long as business was good," and he depended on word of mouth to advertise his display.

This new life, as much as he enjoyed it, was difficult for Fritzy who was not aggressive about meeting strangers. After he caught their attention, though, he was a showman himself, quite humorous and intelligent. Almost everyone who visited Determination asked about the carver, Mooney, and they wanted to know all about him. Fritzy never accepted any credit for the locomotives and he was always eager to describe Mooney and to talk about his life and creations. When Mooney was along, the job was all the easier for Fritzy who preferred the role of advance man and driver. With Mooney out front, Fritzy would settle back in a corner of the truck and observe the visitors and listen to them marvel about his brother's creations.

"How do you do that carving?" someone would ask.

"It's simple," Mooney would explain, quite seriously. "You take a block of wood and you see in it what you want; what you don't want you take away. What you have left is the carving."

Fritzy made a hobby of collecting the exclamations of surprised visitors. "This man must talk to God" was the most unusual comment while "I don't believe it" and "The man's a genius" were most common.

It wasn't often that Mooney was able to accompany his brother, however, and so Fritzy usually ran the show alone, occasionally joined by Tom and later David, who helped entertain the crowds.

By the fall of 1926, Fritzy was comfortable in his new role and he headed south. He was attracted to warm weather and sunny skies, so he followed the fairs and carnivals to Florida and on through Texas and he spent the winter in those southern states. Most winters thereafter, as a matter of fact, were spent in the South. In the spring, Fritzy followed the strawberry festivals north and then west, stopping in Dover for a few days to be with his family. As he expected, the crowds were a bit thinner outside Mooney's home state but Fritzy was philosophical about it — Let the show sell itself, he figured, and it did. It was most advantageous for Mooney to join the tour when it was outside of Ohio as his voice, as

shrieking as a train whistle, and his shock of hair, now white
and as uncontrollable as ever, attracted the attention that
Fritzy's tall, lean body and mild manners could not
command. People would swarm to Determination just to get
a look at the distinctive Yankee. Once, in Texas, a man
approached Mooney and asked if he were an "ordinary
man."

"Yup, I am," said Mooney.

"Can't be," the Texan retorted. "Ya ain't been in town
more 'n an hour and the whole town's buzzin' 'bout ya. Hell, I
lived here all ma' life and they ain't talkin' 'bout me yet."

Any time that Mooney Warther drew a crowd, which was
all the time, he felt compelled to entertain. And, on the road,
free of his workshop and chores, he entertained twelve hours
a day. People weren't satisfied, though, just listening to
Mooney's stories, and Mooney's hands were itchy without
the feel of a knife handle. The tiny, wooden pliers, already
famous in Ohio, satisfied both the carver and his crowds.
Mooney, if he carved hundred of pliers for his playmates in
Dover, carved hundreds of thousands for his visitors and
admirers during his lifetime. As a result of the popularity of
these pliers, Mooney's stereotyped image, since the days of
Determination, has been of him leaning against his truck,
suspenders over his shoulders, bushy head bent forward
studying the block of wood in his busy hands, and all the
while telling a story to his awe-struck crowd. The pliers were
predictably popular on the road, perhaps just as popular as
the locomotives and Mooney himself, though they lacked the
depth of the feature attractions. At first, Mooney gave away
the pliers, but then it struck him that the trinkets could
further his realization of a small museum in Dover.
Thereafter he charged a nickel for them and credited every
cent to his museum fund. Mooney could carve the pliers in
twenty seconds or less and he would boast, "If there are any
shavings when I'm done I'll buy you a new hat and a pair of

shoes to match." Well, he never bought a pair of shoes for anyone, with the exception of himself and members of his family. There were no shavings. Once or twice, perhaps, there were sprinklings of shavings around Mooney's feet after he carved a pair of pliers, but the shavings had been dropped from behind Mooney's back by Fritzy or some other prankster, probably trying to even the score with the master.

Mooney had never forgotten the lesson of the hobo who had introduced him to the wooden pliers and through the years he had improved the hobo's method so that he could produce the pincers by making ten quick slices in a block of wood, one-half inch square and three-and-a-half inches long. It took minimal skill to cut the pliers but a wrong slice, or a long slice, could ruin the finished product or cut off a thumb. Many days Mooney cut between three and four hundred pairs of pliers and often he would wrap a piece of tape around his thumb to protect it.

"Did you cut your thumb?" someone would invariably question.

"Nope," Mooney would say. "I'm a lot smarter than most folks. Most folks cut their fingers and then bandage 'em. *I* bandage mine *before* I cut 'em."

Only once did Mooney need more than twenty seconds to cut a pair of pliers and that was in Hannibal, Missouri, not far from the legendary area of Tom Sawyer and Huckleberry Finn. Mooney blamed the additional two seconds on his knife! Actually, Mooney could cut the pliers in fifteen seconds and his best time was recorded in Shelby, Ohio on September 26, 1935 (by S. P. Shuler) when he produced a pair of pincers in ten seconds. (Those pliers are on display in the Warther museum.)

At the end of a week's work on the road, Mooney may have collected more than $100 worth of nickels, depending on the number of towns and the size of the crowds that week. That cash, combined with coins from the donation box, amounted to a considerable sum of money, but Mooney had devised the perfect safe. The tender of Mooney's model of the Hudson, which was included in the tour, was rigged so that by pressing a certain lump of coal, known only to Mooney and Fritzy, the top of the tender would slide back and expose the empty model. Inside the tender, Mooney and Fritzy stored their cash and other valuables. No one ever suspected their secret and even the best of thieves would have encountered a challenge in cracking the Hudson's safe.

Determination's donation box was split fifty-fifty by Mooney and Fritzy but the nickels that Mooney accumulated from his plier sales were usually mailed Special Delivery in a wooden crate to 331 Karl Avenue. Mooney delighted in watching a postman's puzzled face as he weighed and handled the crate of coins.

"What's inside?" the clerk usually had to know.

"Oh, just a bunch of valuable tools," Mooney would say. In a sense the nickels were tools and within nine years there would be enough of them to build Mooney's first museum.

Since Mooney was unable to travel with Fritzy for more than perhaps two or three times a year, and since Mooney realized the promotional value of the pliers, he taught Fritzy, and later Tom and David, to carve the wooden pincers. Fritzy and his nephews weren't as quick at carving pliers as Mooney, but then they never charged for their pliers. They used them simply to attract the crowds as they traveled from town to town with Determination. When Fritzy finished a pair of pliers, he'd look around the crowd and say, in the direction of a youngster, "You opened your mouth the widest so you can have these pliers." It was a successful gimmick.

In his later years, Fritzy often boasted that while he was on the road for thirty-two years, and visited forty-eight states time and again, he never once had an accident. By 1942, however, after he had driven the Dodge display truck for more than three hundred thousand miles, Fritzy decided he needed a later model and so he and Mooney purchased a Chevrolet. The tour continued through 1959 and more than twelve million persons saw Determination before Fritzy retired from the road.

While Fritzy managed the road tour, Mooney continued to manage his career in Dover. During the Depression, times were extremely difficult for the Warthers, more so because many people in town assumed they had money. Mooney was too proud to tell them otherwise; at the same time, it didn't much matter to him what people thought. Occasionally he knew he was being overcharged for services or materials, but he never questioned a debt or hesitated to pay it. He couldn't tolerate owing money to anyone and his conscience was at ease only when he was debt-free.

When Mooney wasn't traveling with Fritzy or making knives, the latter again being vital to his existence, Mooney continued to carve. He finished the Great Northern in May of 1933 and in October of that year he started another member of the Evolution of the Steam Engine, Cugnot's Steam Carriage, which he completed in about twenty-three days. Cugnot's Steam Carriage had been built in France in 1769 and Cugnot wrecked the three-wheeled vehicle in Paris when he was traveling at a top speed of two-and-a-half miles per hour. After his accident, the inventor was arrested for speeding!

In March of 1934, Mooney began James Watt's Condensing Engine, built in England, 1774. In May, he started Newcomen's Atmospheric Engine, also built in England, but in 1705. The final model that year was begun at the end of October when Mooney carved Branca's Steam Turbine, built in Rome in 1629. The Greek's Whirling Aeolipile, first century A.D., was carved in five days during March, 1935. In September of that year, he carved Hero's Engine in twenty days. Built in Egypt in 250 B.C., Hero's Engine is the first model in Mooney's Evolution of the Steam

Engine. The engine was used to open and close the doors of
Egyptian tombs and many naive Egyptians, unaware of the
hidden engine which was powered by fire that burned in
front of the tombs, believed the idols were actually opening
and closing the doors.

While these models were essential to the evolution of
steam, and while their individual histories were sometimes
fascinating, Mooney was apparently not overly excited
about them. For the most part, he could carve each of the
engines in a matter of a few days and they represented no
challenge for him — not like the Hudson and the great
Northern. Consequently, in Mooney's diaries, there's seldom
any mention of these carvings, except to list the carving time
and the cost of materials.

When Mooney finished Hero's Engine on September 26,
1935, he put down his carving knife and would not pick it up
again for more than two years. During that time it was
difficult for Mooney to acquire the supplies for his carvings,
but in addition to that, he was temporarily preoccupied with
a more immediate project — a museum. Mooney had carved
more than sixty locomotives by 1935. Many of them, those
completed prior to 1913, he had burned or given away. About
twenty of them were on the road with Fritzy. But that left
twenty others for Mooney to display at home where space,
with a growing family, was limited. The Warthers' living
room was a showcase with Mooney's locomotives arranged
about the room, his arrowhead collections decorating the
walls along with various canes and other trinkets, *and*
Frieda's button collections (including eighty thousand
buttons), which she had started mounting during the
Depression. After so many years of displaying the
collections in the front room, the family was accustomed to
their in-house museum. But as Mooney became more popular
and his collections larger, and as more people wanted to see
his models, the living room became an inconvenience.

Hardly a Sunday dinner could be enjoyed at the Warthers' without some family of strangers plodding onto the back porch and pleading to see Mooney and the models. There was no privacy. It's doubtful that Mooney minded the interruptions, though, except if he were working. A Sunday dinner was not all that important to him. If Frieda minded, she never said. The children *did* mind, however, particularly the girls who were teenagers and who valued their privacy. Tom and David gradually became used to the interruptions, but Florence, who was nineteen, Alice, seventeen and Wilma, fifteen, resented the strangers. They also feared that someone might try to burglarize their home for money that wasn't there. And young David, following the kidnapping of the Lindbergh child, often worried that he might be next.

Eventually, when the girls could not find satisfactory work in Dover — the daughters of "wealthy" Mooney Warther certainly didn't need to work — the three girls left home *and* Dover, only to visit Mom and Pop occasionally. Even during their return visits to Dover the girls resented the intruders who by then came in droves and walked and inspected every inch of their childhood home and playground. It seemed so irreverent. Tom and David, however, would remain for life in Dover and for many years both of them worked with their father.

Mooney was not unaware of the uneasiness about his living room showcase. He was sympathetic to the family's inconvenience and long before 1935, he had decided to build a museum as soon as the money was available. A museum, of course, would attract even more strangers to Karl Avenue, but that wasn't Mooney's concern — it was his objective. At least the museum would restore privacy to his home.

The wooden pliers had generated a healthy museum fund by 1935 and so Mooney, assisted by Tom and Jake and several nephews, designed and constructed a one-room museum (twelve feet by eighteen feet) directly behind the

Warther home and across from the grape arbor. Once the museum was built, which required only a few months, Mooney arranged his locomotives along one long wall and opposite his carvings he included rare items from the collection of W. W. Scott, editor and publisher of the Iron Valley Reporter, an early newspaper in Dover. Scott, a veteran of the Civil War, had collected many souvenirs from that era, plus signatures from celebrities and a copy of "My Country 'Tis of Thee," handwritten by its author, the Reverend Samuel Francis Smith. Scott gave his collection to Mooney for safe-keeping. On the same wall with the Scott articles, Mooney also displayed some of his personal momentos, including pliers, postcards from admirers, canes that he had carved in honor of Lincoln and Lindbergh, and letters praising his talent.

Warther's Wonderland, as the museum was initially titled (the name was dropped in later years), was dedicated on May 10, 1936 — Mother's Day. Muti Warther, a spry eighty-six years old, accepted the honor of cutting the ribbon that day during a public ceremony. Perhaps that was Muti's proudest moment as she shared in the success of her talented young son, Ernest. In a sense, it was a celebration of her own success — Mooney Warther, before all else, was a product of this immigrant, once penniless widow who had the stamina to survive, when survival alone was extremely courageous. Two years later, after a long, rewarding and inspiring life, Muti Warther died.

The addition of a museum at 331 Karl Avenue created another flurry of interest as newspapers and radio stations throughout the state publicized the Mother's Day opening. Now, along with the already famous swing in the Calico Ditch, the quaint workshop and the personality of Mooney, not to mention the locomotives, more people than ever before wanted to visit the world's master carver. Mooney's home, however, was not simple to locate. Karl Avenue was a dirt

alley until 1930 when Mooney and his neighbors (after the
city refused to pave it) laid a brick road from in front of his
home, where Karl Avenue ended, out to Tuscarawas Avenue,
a major thoroughfare, where the alley began. Mooney called
the avenue Dumb Street. "The farther down the street you
go, the dumber they get," he used to say, "and I live in the
last house." The day they bricked the alley Mooney's friends
laid a gold brick in front of Mooney's home and made him
the Dean of Dumb Street. Even the Post Office recognized
Dumb Street as a legitimate address and every year,
particularly at Christmas, several cards and letters would be
addressed to "That loud Swiss on Dumb Street."

   To make it easier for visitors to find him and the museum,
particularly out-of-town visitors who were lured to Dover by
Fritzy's tour, Mooney designed and built several signs and
erected them at crucial points in the city, pointing the way to
the world's master carver. Through the years the signs were
improved and replaced. Eventually, even the little museum
was replaced by a larger, modern building. Mooney Warther
had guessed correctly. Americans, even foreign visitors,
wanted to see the Evolution of the Steam Engine and talk
with its creator. But Mooney had never dreamed their
interest would outlive his lifetime.

Chapter Nine

The War Years

"If God had made everyone Swiss," Mooney Warther used to philosophize, "there'd be plenty of good cheese, lots of beer and no wars." The thought was meant to amuse Mooney's crowds but it was not entirely in jest. War was anathema to Mooney Warther. He could not understand it. Killing a human being was unconscionable to him, unless in self defense. Even anger was to be avoided in the Warther household. "Getting mad destroys the mind mentally and physically too," Mooney often preached to his children. "It takes more effort to get mad than to fix what you're mad about." Mooney practiced his preaching and there's hardly anyone who ever witnessed him in a fit of anger. Not that he didn't get angry — he certainly did — but he vented his frustrations privately and non-violently.

Mooney was cognizant of the implications of war. Wars improved economies, but that was no excuse. They (sometimes) settled disputes — still no excuse. Wars maimed and killed. Mooney had lost his closest friend, Johnny Richard, in World War I, and the best of economies or even the best of worlds could not be traded for that friendship. Mooney had not forgotten Johnny Richard when in the early 1940s the United States entered World War II. At that time, Mooney was recuperating from a broken back which he had sustained in a fall from his famous swing. (Ironically Mooney was the only person ever to be seriously injured on the swing, and he was nearly paralyzed. Four vertebrae were crushed in the carver's back and doctors said he might never walk again. But Mooney was too stubborn, too intent on living, to allow a broken back to interfere with his plans. The Evolution of the Steam Engine remained to be completed and Mooney could not carve it from bed. He walked in a matter of months but he had back trouble for years thereafter, though few people were aware of it.) Shortly before his tragic fall, Mooney had completed another member of the Evolution of the Steam Engine, that being the B & O Constant Steam Torque. Mooney finished his model in 1938 and it was the first engine added to his project since 1935, when he had carved the whirling Aeolipile and Hero's Engine. Several crucial locomotive models remained to be carved and the carver was growing impatient about completing his project. But when the United States entered the second world war, Mooney's project was shelved once again. With the exception of an ivory model of the General, completed in 1942, Mooney would not carve another model before 1947. World War II, despite Mooney's feelings about it, prevented him from carving. His knife business enjoyed an unbidden prosperity during the war and required every minute of his time.

When a young man in Tuscarawas County packed his bags and left for war, the craftsmanship of Mooney Warther was not overlooked. Mooney's knives had long been in demand by housewives and gift-givers but now they were needed to fulfill a most begrudging duty. Mooney was overwhelmed with orders from soldiers, wives of soldiers, parents of soldiers and friends of soldiers who wanted their loved ones to be armed with a fearsome, penetrating knife. Mooney's decision to fill the orders required considerable reflection. On one hand, he needed the money. The opening of his museum in 1936 provided some additional income, but even that added to his share of the road show's profit was barely sufficient to meet his family's obligations, and to

purchase materials for the Evolution of the Steam Engine.
Luxuries, so commonplace just ten years earlier, were
impossible and Frieda's frugal management, as it had been
through the thirties, was crucial.

On the other hand, would he be furthering the war effort
and contradicting his convictions if he obliged the many
servicemen who sought his knives? Some folks would say so,
but then that wouldn't matter to Mooney. He would not
contribute to the continuation of the war, but he would make
thousands of servicemen secure knowing they had a Mooney
Warther knife at hand. At the same time he would improve
his financial status. The war would not create a second
Golden Era for Mooney and his family — that would be
contradictory, even shameful — it would only ease their
burden.

The popularity of Mooney's war knives, which he called
Commando Knives, mushroomed in the early months of the
war when a serviceman's wife asked the cutler to make her
husband a seven-inch, two-edged knife with a heavy sheath.
After Mooney made the knife and the serviceman had
received it, he was so satisfied that he ordered a half-dozen
additional knives for his friends. His friends ordered knives
for their friends. Then, several stores around the country
heard about what one serviceman tagged the "best knives in
the United States Army" and Mooney received orders for a
dozen, or twenty or thirty knives at a time. The requests from
Tuscarawas County alone were sufficient to keep Mooney
busy six days a week and eventually he asked Fritzy to stop
the road show for a year or more and lend his hand at the
knifeshop. He also hired Johnny Meese, a nephew who lived
next door on Karl Avenue.

It took half-a-day to make just one Commando Knife but
when it was finished the owner knew he possessed a reliable,
enviable weapon. A seven-inch, double-edged Commando
Knife earned $18 for Mooney; a standard eight-inch knife,

$20; the B-29 eight-inch, $25; the Mae West, eight-inch $30; and ivory handles cost $10 extra. For the extravagant, there was a $100 model!

It's not certain how many Commando Knives Mooney and his cutlers made during World War II, but the number would be in the thousands. He did number many of the knives and in his diary he recorded the sales of two of them: "Knives that were sold after the number 300," he wrote. "Knife number 301 sold to H. J. Lemcke, Webster Grove, Mo. Knife number 302 sold to F. C. Welliver, Missouri." Knifemaking didn't leave much time for diary writing, however, and Mooney didn't record the sales thereafter. He was always interested, though, in knowing who would possess his knives, and when he had the opportunity he would ask. A customer entered the workshop one afternoon from Indiana and ordered a specially designed, seven-inch Commando.

"Who's it for?" Mooney inquired as he wrote out the order.

"General Mark Clark," the man replied. "He's in the Italian Theatre."

Johnny Meese was fascinated that the Commando Knife he was making would eventually be used by General Clark. To commemorate the event Johnny made an identical ivory-handled knife for himself and then he made a letter opener in the fashion of the Clark knife and later gave it to his wife.

Before Fritzy came off the road during the war, Johnny was Mooney's only assistant and they shared a friendship similar to that of Mooney and Johnny Richard or of Mooney and Tom Moore. There was a difference of twenty-three years between Mooney and his sister's son, but there was no generation gap. Mooney was always a youngster at heart and Johnny was a mature, determined worker. Of course, he wasn't afraid to tease Mooney, for as a boy, when he was part of that most famous neighborhood gang, Johnny had learned that Mooney enjoyed practical jokes. More than once during the war years, Johnny crept into Mooney's shop

in the early morning hours and turned Mooney's hacksaw
blade upside down. Mooney was amused by the pranks and
relished Johnny's participation in the many little games
that were part of Mooney's life — crazy, fun games; relaxing
games.

One game was played every workday afternoon, without
fail. It was a sort-of ritual. About four o'clock, Mooney would
begin to close the shop and he'd tell Johnny, "I'm going
outside to throw the brick in the air. If it comes down, we'll go
for a beer. If it doesn't, we'll stay and work."

All but once the brick came down. The exception occurred
on the day that Johnny threw the brick. He had rigged wire
around the red block of clay so that when he tossed it in the
air it caught on Frieda's clothesline and would not fall to the
ground. And that day, true to the rules, Mooney and Johnny
returned to the shop and worked an additional hour.

The other days, however, after the brick had hit the ground
and the workshop door was locked, Mooney and Johnny
hopped on their bicycles and peddled to Leonard's or some
other tavern in the downtown vicinity and enjoyed a mug of
beer. "Listen for their buzzin'," Mooney would instruct his
nephew as they neared a tavern. "If there's buzzin' there's
beer; if there's not, let's move on." Occasionally it was
difficult for the taverns to get beer but Leonard's, owned and
operated by Leonard Contini, was usually well stocked and
the bar overflowed with thirsty laborers, many of them
former millmen, who had stopped for their afternoon ale.
The scene was always one of great congeniality and
everyone, of course, knew Mooney Warther. And, as could be
expected, he was usually the highlight of the afternoon with
his latest tales and games. As a result, Mooney and Leonard
became good friends and the stout tavern owner always
looked forward to Mooney's visits.

Mooney committed what he called "the dumbest stunt of
all" at Leonard's one afternoon. Before stopping for a beer

this particular day, Mooney rode his Cadillac to Lawrence Carmola's shoe store on Tuscarawas Avenue in Dover's business section and purchased a pair of penny loafers. Enroute to Leonard's he also stopped at Eiler's Candy Shop, also in the business district, where he purchased a quart of homemade ice cream, prepared by his neighbor, Henry Eiler. Then, on to Leonard's. It was a warm afternoon and so Mooney asked Leonard if he could store his ice cream in the tavern's large, walk-in freezer while he enjoyed a fishbowl of beer. Of course Leonard agreed. Mooney mingled with his friends and talked about the events of the day for about an hour, all the while enjoying his fishbowl. Then, he grabbed his package from the freezer and went for his bicycle, where he had left his package of shoes — or what he thought were his shoes. He had stored the shoes in the freezer and left the ice cream to melt in the basket of his Cadillac! Mooney roared with laughter and the commotion drew several of Leonard's customers outside to see what was so funny. Mooney showed them the melted ice cream and to make up for the loss, he went back inside the tavern for another fishbowl. Neither Leonard nor Mooney would ever forget the incident and they laughed about it for years thereafter as they recounted the story time and again for various customers.

Many of Mooney's anecdotes were told at Leonard's. A favorite, in addition to the "dumbest stunt of all," was the time Mooney tried to make bracciolas, an Italian specialty. He had bet an Italian friend that he could prepare a better dish of bracciola. Leonard, an accomplished Italian cook, would sample the dish and determine the winner, who would be awarded a keg of beer. Mooney's problem, however, was that he didn't know how to cook bracciolas and so Leonard coached him. "It's similar to frying steak but it's not the same," Leonard explained and he told Mooney how to fix the dish. On the day of the contest, Mooney was left alone to make his bracciolas. He seasoned the thin slices of steak, just as Leonard had instructed him, fried and rolled each piece of steak and tied it with a string. But, instead of dropping the steak into spaghetti sauce, as he had been told, Mooney, perhaps absent-mindedly, set the steak in Frieda's oven and baked it. In the meantime, his attention was diverted and the pieces of steak roasted until they looked like chunks of charcoal. Mooney was embarrassed and of course he couldn't enter the contest so he rode his Cadillac to the local brewery and purchased a keg of beer...Then, at Leonard's, he helped consume the beer along with his friend's tasty platter of bracciolas. Thereafter, Mooney never attempted to make bracciolas. "If you can't be the best, don't do it," Mooney often said, and there were plenty of others who knew how to fix bracciolas better than he.

On many afternoons during the war years, when it was muggy and uncomfortable, Mooney and Johnny bought a pack of beer at Leonard's and carried it back to Karl Avenue where they and several friends enjoyed the ale that evening under the grape arbor. On those trips Mooney insisted that he and Johnny share the load of carrying the package — halfway for each man. And just to make certain that Johnny carried his share, Mooney once stepped off every foot between his home and Leonard's door. Seventh Street was half-way.

Mooney Warther never overlooked an opportunity for fun — even in his business operations. One day Robert Ohio Weible, a staunch Republican, came into Mooney's shop and ordered a Commando Knife. He was a tall, heavy man who constantly flicked a cigar between his lips. Mooney knew Weible and his political leanings and mockingly carved Franklin Delano Roosevelt into the ivory handle of the knife. Weible "blew his top" when he saw it, Mooney later revealed, and Mooney immediately replaced the ivory and cut his customer's name into it.

Mooney's pranks were often played on members of his neighborhood. Henry Eiler, the candy maker, planted a yielding garden to provide fresh vegetables for his family of five children. Every summer, however, just when the tomatoes ripened, Mooney sneaked into Henry's backyard in the early morning and snatched the first ripe tomato. After a couple of seasons Henry caught on to the neighborhood thief, but he was never able to catch Mooney in the act. Nonetheless, Henry and Mooney were great friends who often called on one another when they needed help around their homes. It shocked an occasional onlooker, however, when Mooney requested Henry's help and then afterwards, instead of thanking his friend, he'd shout, "Now go to hell." That was just Mooney Warther, and fortunately, Henry Eiler was amused by him and understood.

Another neighbor who fell victim to Mooney's pranks was old George Knupfher, a widower. George was a loveable old man who was loved by everyone on Karl Avenue. In the winter months, George would get out his snow shovel and remove the snow and ice from the walks along the avenue. In return for his good deed George expected a shot of whiskey, which he guzzled down before moving on to the next home. Fortunately, there were only six homes on Karl Avenue, as George was always out shoveling, even sweeping, after the slightest snowfall.

George was perfect for Mooney's pranks. The old man didn't catch on very fast, and, when he did, he didn't mind. In fact, he appreciated the attention and Mooney gave him plenty of it. Once when George's cornfield was tall and mature, Mooney crept into it after dark, removed the ears of corn and replaced them with bottles of beer. George was ecstatic the next morning when he went corn picking!

In George's potato patch Mooney dug up a mound of potatoes and buried several bottles of beer in their place. Every so often, however, instead of a bottle of beer, Mooney drove a wooden stake into the ground. On top of the stake he nailed a cap from a beer bottle A few days later, Mooney and Johnny watched old George as he dug in the potato patch. He shoved his potato hook into the ground and scooped out a bottle of beer. The old man looked at it inquisitively and then moved to another spot. Another bottle of beer. Quickly, then, he moved to the next spot where his hook caught a snag. George strained to pull up what he thought was another bottle of beer but he was too weak for the buried stake. Eventually he grabbed a shovel and dug up the stake and then he knew Mooney Warther had been in his patch.

On Christmas Eve Mooney and Johnny and several of their friends and neighbors waited for George to go downtown for his evening's beer. Then they entered his home and decorated the living room, complete with Christmas tree and presents. When George returned he cried, he was so happy. It was Mooney's way of making up for all those pranks. Mooney also shaved George once a week, trimmed his hair, and paid him two dollars for the honor.

Pranks were as necessary in Mooney Warther's life as golf and tennis are necessary today in the lives of so many men and women. Through the war years the pranks were particularly necessary to break up the boredom of the work and the workshop. Grinding knife blades could be compared to shearing steel — it wasn't very creative — and assembling knives on a hot afternoon could be just as bothersome as laboring in the American Sheet and Tin Plate Company. But when the orders were there, Mooney felt compelled to produce. An occasional problem, though, was a scarcity of metal and every so often Mooney would fall behind in filling the orders. Some customers were so determined to have a Commando Knife, however, that they supplied their own metal!

Once in the spring of 1944 when Mooney had difficulty

buying metal for his knives, a city slicker of a salesman, by the name of Charlie Going, visited Mooney and offered to sell his knives on the road. Mooney wasn't interested. Charlie attracted the cutler's attention, however, when he offered to deliver a truckload of scrap metal to 331 Karl Avenue. Charlie was fascinated by Mooney, his family, and by Mooney's museum and carvings, so he was willing to rent a truck and haul the metal to Dover. On the day of the delivery Mooney was gratified by Charlie's kindness and in appreciation he offered Charlie a spare bedroom for the evening. After one evening with Charlie Going, another Mooney Warther friendship had been struck, and the bedroom became Charlie's weekend haven for many years. In effect, he became a part of the Warther family, but he earned his way.

Charlie realized as well as Mooney that when the war ended, the lucrative Commando Knife business would cease with it. And then, Mooney would need another income, as the post-war years would be economically difficult. The museum had potential as a money-maker, but it never generated more than $200 a year before 1947. Some months, especially during the winters, donations at the museum were as little as $1.90. The road show provided an almost healthy income but it was divided evenly between Fritzy and Mooney. In 1942, for example, the truck grossed $2,346.42 but approximately $700 of that was subtracted for expenses, including insurance, gasoline, electricity, a license and repairs.

Mooney confided in Charlie that he was concerned about his financial future and Charlie's creative mind was set in motion. Charlie urged Mooney to take himself to the people, in the fashion of Determination, but on a grander scale. He suggested that Mooney build a larger museum, perhaps away from Karl Avenue where it would attract more people. And he also urged Mooney to advertise and sell his kitchen

cutlery throughout the country. Mooney wasn't convinced.
He was still small-town Mooney Warther and Charlie Going
was talking like one of those New York Central
representatives. Granted, Mooney had nothing to fear of a
New York Central type, but he wasn't convinced. "Maybe I
will," Mooney responded to Charlie's suggestions, but when
Mooney said "maybe" that meant the idea required a lot of
thinking.

The thinking came sooner than Mooney had anticipated.
He was making a Commando Knife in mid-August, 1945
when he heard the news that the war had ended. He stopped
immediately, as he had always said he would, and never
finished the knife. (Today it hangs, unfinished, in his
workshop in Dover.) Mooney went on "a little toot" as V-J
Day deserved a celebration. For it meant not only the end of
a dreadful war, but that Mooney Warther, the carver, was
free to carve again.

Chapter Ten

April 7, 1947

Charlie Going was a savvy promoter who became the renaissance man in Mooney Warther's career. By 1946, the Warthers had accepted Charlie as a member of their family and employed him in the knife business which returned to producing kitchen and steak knives following the war. David came home from the service that year and he and his brother, Tom, assumed the responsibilities of knife-making and freed their father to complete the Evolution of the Steam Engine. Charlie assisted the Warther boys but all the while his mind was on a more detailed, encompassing project that involved Mooney and his carvings. Charlie had not succeeded in convincing Mooney to take his Evolution of the Steam Engine "off the hill," as Karl Avenue was referred to, but he *had* interested Mooney in a country-wide publicity campaign that would attract millions of viewers and simultaneously earn a living for not only the carver, but also his promoter who received a commission.

To stimulate business in the late 1940s, America's department stores searched for promotions that would ease their customers out of a war mood and into a less serious attitude. Mooney's display of locomotives, along with Mooney himself, would be perfect for twenty-six of the largest department stores in the country. Charlie arranged the promotion which went on tour in 1947 and continued through 1952.

The kick-off for the promotion began in Dover, actually,

but not in a department store. The City of Dover had never honored Mooney Warther and by 1947 many members of the Chamber of Commerce were embarrassed by this fact, though Mooney thought nothing of it. He didn't expect any tributes. Nonetheless, Charlie worked with the Chamber and on April 7, 1947, six hundred of Mooney's friends gathered at St. John's United Church of Christ (where Mooney had met Frieda many years before) to honor Dover's — and the world's — master carver. City and state officials, prominent citizens, industrialists, former millmen, as well as neighbors and family, were there for the testimonial. Mooney, with Frieda at his side, was overwhelmed by the event. The surprise that evening was a handsome plaque with a photograph of Mooney engraved above this paragraph of praise:

TO

ERNEST (MOONEY) WARTHER

We, the citizens of Dover, proudly join hands in honoring
you as the world's greatest carver.
Your priceless collection of model masterpieces not only
has given this city a rich endowment, but also has
endeared you to the hearts of all your fellow citizens.

Presented by
THE DOVER CHAMBER OF COMMERCE

April 7, 1947

When Mooney was presented the plaque, he stood to acknowledge his appreciation but when he opened his mouth there was only silence. Mooney was speechless and emotional as he considered the plaque the greatest honor that any man could receive. He sat down, teary-eyed, and smiled at his friends.

The next morning Mooney visited the editor of the Dover Daily Reporter and asked him to print the remarks which he was too awe-struck to deliver the evening before. Along with the newspaper's account of the testimonial, the editor included Mooney's thank you. It read:

It is beyond any words of mine to express my sincere appreciation of that which is being done here tonight for me and mine. It is far beyond my fondest dream, when I think of the humble beginning and the many years that I have carved not for money or for glory, but for the sheer love of the work, a work that has long ago taken me from the steel mills, a work that has been admired by many millions of people throughout the land. Fortunes have I refused. Now I am being honored by my own community, and when a man is honored by his own community and lives to see it, be that community large or small, it is as great an honor as can be bestowed upon any man. My spirit and ambition are as great as ever, and I long to carry on the work until I lay down my knife for the last time and leave behind a piece of work that will be admired by all the world."

April, 1947, was the month of testimonials as the week following the Chamber's event, (and probably sparked by that event) the Dover High School newspaper headlined Mooney Warther as Dover's Number One Citizen. After Mooney read the newspaper story, written by high school students, he remarked, "I can add to my work, but never can a higher honor come to me. This is the top of my career." He referred not only to the newspaper account, but also to the events of April 7, 1947.

During the next several years Mooney (and Charlie) traveled from one large city to the next entertaining department store audiences. His pattern was to appear at a department store for a one-to-two week promotion, never less than one week, and in-between he spent several weeks in Dover carving the Evolution of the Steam Engine or working on other projects. He also took time to join Fritzy with the road show now and then, especially during the summer months when Fritzy looked forward to his own time off. Of course, Fritzy always met Mooney and Charlie at the department stores as Determination carried the fifteen models that were displayed during the promotions. Mooney didn't want to disturb the models in his museum on Karl Avenue.

In return for the $2,500 weekly fee which the department stores paid to Mooney Warther, they were treated to a profitable promotion that attracted not only customers, but television cameras, newspaper reporters and magazine writers. The response to Mooney, as it had been in the early 1920s on the Service Progress Special, was resounding. In Hartford, Connecticut, for example, despite a treacherous blizzard, school children lined up outside the department store where Mooney was scheduled to appear. In addition to the children, a community of Swiss traveled twenty snow-covered miles that day just to greet one of their own. The resulting story topped any of the day's news events, including the record-setting blizzard, and newspapers, radio and television stations responded with generous coverage.

It was that way practically everywhere that Mooney Warther appeared, and he had grown accustomed to it. Fortunately he never tired of it. Nor did he tire of the people, their comments, and their attitudes. The department store tour, in fact, added to Mooney's repertoire of stories and episodes. His favorite department store incident occurred in

Bloomingdale's, twenty-five years to the day after he had first appeared in New York's Grand Central Station.

A fashionable woman with a fur piece around her shoulders and a chauffeur as her escort, stepped up to Mooney at the end of his first day there and asked, "Mister, you look happy and healthy, but tell me, are you rich?"

"Yep, I am." Mooney's voice echoed throughout the store. "I'm the richest man in the world. My roof don't leak, my family's not hungry, and I don't owe anybody. Yep, I'm the richest man in the world and I can prove it." He handed her the 1947 plaque from the Chamber of Commerce.

She read it, glanced at Mooney and said, "Yes, Mr. Warther, I guess you are the richest man in the world." And she walked away.

Mooney Warther was happiest in front of a crowd, be it his family, his contemporaries, the neighborhood children, or strangers. And when Mooney was happiest, he was also most productive. The department store tour of the late 1940s and the early 1950s was precisely the motivation he needed to complete the Evolution of the Steam Engine. But first, he decided to carve a project that he had wanted to perfect for more than thirty years. On three occasions, including two in the early years of his life, Mooney had carved a wooden model of the steel mill where he had worked for nearly twenty-five years. His most recent re-creation of the American Sheet and Tin Plate Company was completed shortly before World War II, but Mooney was not satisfied with the model. He wanted the carving to include two mills, powered by electricity, in addition to a dozen or more millmen whom he wanted to remember from those days. So in 1948, not long after he carved a third model of the 999, Mooney began his fourth steel mill. The carving dates for the steel mill are not known, but Mooney re-created it from memory. Then, he included it with Determination so that it could be shown on the road and in department stores. This, however, left Mooney's museum without a steel mill, so in 1952 he carved the fifth, and final, replica of the American Sheet and Tin Plate Co. And it's a masterpiece. The 1948 model was carved in walnut and maple, but in 1952 Mooney carved in ivory and walnut. The last model included two mills, operated by seventeen neatly posed millmen, characterized realistically by the master carver. Underneath the model Mooney placed a mirror to reflect the electrically powered wheels and belts that set the mills and the millmen in motion. Mooney displayed the steel mill in his workshop because his museum was already overcrowded. There he gathered his visitors around the four sides of the waist-high model and explained the mill and told the people a true story about each millman who had worked with him in the years prior to the Service Progress Special.

"But where are you?" some youngsters would always want to know.

"Ain't there," Mooney would boom. "I couldn't find ivory hard enough to carve my head."

With the completion of the 1952 steel mill, Mooney channeled his energy to the Evolution of the Steam Engine. In 1933 the carver had prematurely written in his diary that he had completed the project, but then he decided there were several significant models that must be included. He had finished the ivory General in 1942, just before he was swamped with orders for Commando Knives. Since the war, he had completed a 999, on May 12, 1948, and then in early 1950 (the exact dates are not known) he carved the Stourbridge Lion, which was built in England in 1829 and later transported to the United States. The actual engine was later consigned to the Smithsonian Institution.

Mooney had completed these latter models in his off weeks during the department show tour. But in 1953, when he decided to carve the final member of the Evolution of the Steam Engine, Mooney set aside all other projects and refused interruptions. This final member required his intent concentration and every bit of his energy.

In 1941 the Union Pacific Railroad had introduced the Big Boy, the climax of steam locomotives in America. It was the most daring built — one hundred thirty-four feet long, six hundred four tons, twenty-eight thousand horsepower — and designed to the widest and highest maximums to get the engine through tunnels, under bridges and around curves. The American Locomotive Works built twenty-five Big Boys.

Mooney began the model on January 13 and spent several hours a day, every day except Sundays, carving the model. Fortunately, there was no urgency about Mooney's earning an income as nowadays only he and Frieda were at home and they continued to live modest lives. Mooney had managed to save money during the department store tour, the road show continued to contribute a steady income and now the museum was showing a healthy profit. In 1947, at the start of the department store tour, the museum had earned only $207.90, but in 1948, when Mooney's name was being broadcast and headlined across the country, the museum took in $765.95. In 1950 the museum provided Mooney with $977 and after 1951 the museum grossed in excess of $1,000 annually. Of course, much of the money was earned during the spring and summer months — some months brought in more than $200 — but Mooney knew to save the money for the winter, when the income might be as little as $20 in December and January.

Mooney did entertain the many visitors to his museum during 1953 — that was necessary to relax him and charge his enthusiasm — but he carved in the pre-dawn hours before any visitors were likely to arrive. Progress on the sixty-six inch model, which required seven thousand parts, was invigorating and consequently Mooney said he enjoyed carving the Big Boy more than any of the forty-one members

that preceded it. Of course, his emotions were mixed. The Big
Boy was the final member of the Evolution of the Steam
Engine, and since Mooney intended to retire, he believed the
Big Boy would also be his last carving. No doubt he felt an
occasional twinge of sadness mixed with regret as he
dressed in the early mornings and walked to his workshop.
The Evolution of the Steam Engine, after all, had been his
enviable and renowned project for forty years. But if there
were any thoughts of delaying the Big Boy, Mooney ignored
them. He was ardent about finishing the model. Once he
began carving in the mornings, he rarely left his workshop
and one day he carved for seventeen-and-a-half hours! By
then, however, sentiment governed the carver's hands. If the
Big Boy were to be his final carving, then he would complete
it on a special day. Therefore, Mooney scheduled his time so
that on October 30, 1953 — his sixty-eighth birthday — he
cut the finishing slice into the burly Big Boy. It was a proud
and fulfilling moment. The Evolution of the Steam Engine
was complete. And, for now, Mooney's carving career had
come to an end. Mooney felt the same sensations on October
30 that he had felt on April 7, 1947. It was a grand day — not
only for Mooney, the carver, but also for American history.

Ironically, at about the time Mooney celebrated the
completion of the Evolution of the Steam Engine, the steam
locomotive in America puffed its departing breath of smoke.
Subsequently it was replaced by a more efficient and
economical diesel engine. Mooney had no desire to carve a
diesel, however. "They're uglier than a tomato worm," he'd
say. "They take the romance out of railroading" and there'd
be no romance between Mooney Warther and a diesel.

Chapter Eleven

Mooney's World

Throughout his life Mooney often said, "Think you can and start. Never pretend anyone is trying to stop you or hinder you. Give the people enough of what they want and they will keep you. They poisoned Socrates, crucified Christ and shot Lincoln — well, you can't please all the people." In the years following the completion of the Evolution of the Steam Engine, Mooney Warther gave the people what they wanted. He pleased the people, and the people kept him. They came from across America and from fourteen foreign countries to listen to his tales and examine his priceless collection of steam locomotives.

Now that his life's project was complete, Mooney had more free time than ever before. He spent it assembling knives, rearranging and mounting his extensive arrowhead collection, and most of all, entertaining the visitors to his museum. On a good Sunday afternoon, for example, he was likely to meet more than a hundred strangers in his backyard and he treated every one of them as a friend. He'd tell them how he had found the pocketknife on the dusty road that led to the pasture and how he had started whittling on sticks and bones. He'd talk about the steel mill and show them his model of it with the tiny millmen. He'd explain his locomotives and enhance their histories with humorous anecdotes. And everyone listened, including restless children and exhausted adults, captivated by this old man in suspenders whose hair was so white and wild, whose stories

were better than Walt Disney's and whose laugh was
resounding and contagious. At seventy years of age, Mooney
Warther was the grandfather of showmen.

By 1956, however, Mooney's hands felt an itch that only a
knife handle could reach. His life was far from over, his mind
was sharp and his senses keen, and his talent for carving in
wood had not deteriorated. He decided he must carve again.
The problem, though, was determining what to carve. It had
been so simple and obvious for him to begin the Evolution of
the Steam Engine in 1913, but now that that was complete,
Mooney found it difficult to define a second project. At first
he decided to carve freak locomotives in American history
and so on June 12, 1956, with feverish enthusiasm, Mooney
began the Stevens Type of the Camden and Amboy (New
Jersey) Railroad. John Stevens designed this engine as a
high speed passenger train, and while the locomotive was
operable, it was powerless and therefore unsuccessful. The
carving was completed on September 3, 1956.

While Mooney was carving the Stevens Type, he was able
to put his project into better focus and he decided to carve the
Epics of Railroad History. It was another natural. As a
history buff, Mooney had often relished accounts of
American history which involved steam locomotives. The
driving of the golden spike, Abraham Lincoln's funeral,the
story of Casey Jones — all of these and several others
featured steam locomotives — and Mooney felt compelled to
re-create the events and preserve their significance in
American history.

His second member was the Nashville, one of four
locomotives which pulled Abraham Lincoln's funeral train
across the country in 1865. The journey took nineteen days
and required a different engine about every five days. The
Nashville led the train through Ohio. Mooney carved the
model between October 1, 1956 and February 1, 1957.

In 1957 Mooney's project was interrupted when he

discovered cracks in the ebony wheels of the locomotives in his Evolution of the Steam Engine. As the ebony aged it became apparent to Mooney that it would eventually break and so he spent the remainder of 1957, after he had completed the Nashville, replacing the ebony with ivory.

In August 1958 Mooney continued the Epics of Railroad History when he began carving The Great Locomotive Chase. The project required ten months carving time and it includes the General, the Yonah, the Texas, three men and one handcar. The eighty-seven-mile chase occurred during the Civil War when Andrews' Raiders stole the General outside Atlanta. The engine pulled supplies for the Confederates and was one of the South's most prized locomotives. Andrews' Raiders headed north with the General and planned to destroy the railroad behind them to Chatanooga. A gang of Confederates, seeing that their engine was being stolen, pursued the Yankee thieves on foot; then by handcar; then by the Yonah, a small, powerless engine; and finally via the Texas, a freighter which was traveling south. The Texas could move faster backwards than the Yonah could forwards so the southerners gave chase in reverse gear.

Andrews' Raiders would have succeeded in their attempt except that they fed the General a load of wet wood, thereby losing speed. Mooney loved to tell this story and he did it with gusto, particularly when he got to the part about Abraham Lincoln awarding Andrews' Raiders the Congressional Medal of Honor.

In August of 1959, Mooney began The Driving of the Golden Spike, a story that rivals that of The Great Locomotive Chase. This carving, completed in May of 1960, includes two locomotives and three men and represents America's first transcontinental railroad. The Union Pacific Railroad, with the 119, left Nebraska traveling west and the Central Pacific, with the Jupiter, left San Francisco going east. The object was to unite the country by rail and in the process see which rail line could lay the most track. Wherever the two lines met, they would tie down the final rail with a golden spike.

The Union Pacific was at a disadvantage with a more mountainous terrain and to make matters worse the Central Pacific recruited a crew of Chinese who could run with the rails and lay more than ten miles of track a day. When the lines met at Promontory Point, Utah, in May, 1869, the Central Pacific had won. Mooney's re-creation shows the driving of the golden spike was witnessed by an Indian; Leland Stanford, the president of the Central Pacific and former governor of California; and Ulysses S. Grant, then president of the United States, whom Mooney portrayed puffing on a cigar. Mooney's story claimed that Stanford, a tall man in a top hat, was given the first swing at the golden spike ... and he missed!

After Mooney had completed the project a visitor informed him that President Grant was not at the scene that day. Mooney thought a moment and studied his caricature of Grant. "Well," quipped the carver, "he should have been," and he let him stay.

Mooney loved the New York Central's 999 Empire State Express, and on one of the final days of 1960 he decided to fulfill a lifelong dream. The 999 first attracted Mooney's attention in 1893 when he was eight years old and the engine set a speed record of one hundred twelve miles per hour. Mooney had always wanted to carve the locomotive in its entirety — he had carved the engine and tender four times by 1960 — and so on December 21 he began the engine, tender and four coaches. To make the model even more appealing than his other carvings, Mooney cut the 999 in ivory and as a result it is the world's largest ivory carving in motion. The 999, with fifteen thousand parts, and a plush, red velvet interior, was completed on December 26, 1961. Mooney was seventy-six years old.

The completion of the ivory 999 generated another flurry of activity on Karl Avenue. Mooney's model was photographed for newspapers and magazines, including *True,* the widely circulated men's publication. Soon thereafter he appeared on Cleveland's Mike Douglas Show where he met comedian and TV-personality Henry Morgan who later arranged for Mooney to appear with him on the Johnny Carson Show in 1965.

Morgan was astonished by Mooney's talent and he was drawn to the carver's personality and subsequently to his museum. The celebrity, who was a panelist on "I've Got A Secret," told Mooney that he collected chess sets, and in 1966 Morgan was called to Dover where Mooney presented him a beautifully cut chessboard and thirty-two chessmen, designed as boiler firemen, smokestack queens, oiler kings, bell bishops and lantern knights. The chessmen were cut in ebony and ivory and the set was valued at "several thousand dollars." When Morgan saw the set he sighed, cast his head from side to side and said, "I don't believe it ... I don't know what to say."

He challenged Mooney to a game and Mooney accepted, though he admitted his ignorance of chess. Nevertheless, a crowd gathered as the two stars moved the unique chessmen across the checkered board which had been outlined in mother-of-pearl.

"You're not winning but you're not losing, either," Morgan chided his friend during one of the most publicized events staged in Dover.

By the early 1960s, Mooney's tiny museum, which was too small the day he dedicated it, was no longer sufficient to house his carvings and accommodate the nearly one hundred thousand visitors who were arriving on Karl

Avenue every year by the bus loads. Mooney was forced to look for a grander showplace.

The Evolution of the Steam Engine, the Epics of Railroad History and the various memorabilia that Mooney had carved, could easily have been crated and shipped to the Smithsonian Institution (whose officials said the carvings were "priceless") or to some resort museum where they might possibly be viewed by millions of persons annually. But that would not occur. Mooney Warther always recognized that *he* belonged in Dover, and since he had created them in Dover, his carvings would remain in Dover. Mooney discussed the possibility of donating his creations to the city library or the Dover Historical Society, but neither of those organizations had the space to accept and display the collections. So Mooney, along with son David who spearheaded the project, decided to build a new museum in his own back yard.

Bruce Mears and Bill Shell, two energetic Dover Jaycees, realized that Mooney's fiftieth anniversary of carving to scale (one-half inch to the foot) would be celebrated in 1963, the same year Mooney planned to open a new museum. They decided it would be appropriate for the Dover Jaycees to sponsor a city-wide promotion in honor of the world's master carver.

They contacted David Warther and informed him of their plans, which had been approved by the Jaycees. Their idea was to organize a Mooney Warther Day to be held in conjunction with the dedication of the new museum. During the celebration, the Jaycees planned to surprise Mooney, and Dover, with a bronze bust of the master carver. Since it was to be a surprise, Mooney could not sit for the bust, and so David arranged for the wife of the Cleveland sculptor who would create the bust, to photograph Mooney without his becoming suspicious. David told his father the sculptor had been hired to make a cast of his hands, and while the photographer snapped Mooney's hands, she also captured his facial expressions and profiles. Mooney, naturally, didn't object to the extra poses.

In the meantime, the two Jaycees set out to raise $1,200 to pay for the bust. Within a day it was obvious to Mears and Shell that raising the money for a bust of Mooney Warther would be the most effortless task of their project. The area's major industries contributed to the fund and urged the Jaycees to expand Mooney Warther Day to include additional promotions. Overnight, Mooney Warther Day became Mooney Warther Week, set for June 8, 1963.

On that day, two thousand persons filled Mooney Warther's back yard to witness the ribbon cutting ceremonies at a modern, $35,000 museum. The building was attached to Mooney's chalet-like workshop and sprawled over one corner of his back yard. Inside, in glass enclosed showcases, he arranged the Evolution of the Steam Engine in one large room, and adjacent to it he displayed the Epics of Railroad History, which now included Casey Jones' Engine, completed just two months before the museum opened. More than sixty locomotives were arranged in the museum, including some duplicates from the road show which had been terminated in 1956. Mooney decorated the museum's walls with his canes and Lincoln plaques and there was room for his Plier Tree, his 1952 model of the Steel Mill, and a display of his carving knives and blades. Best of all, there was ample room for Mooney's thousands of visitors.

The week following the museum's dedication was full of *Mooney Warther Sellabrations* as the downtown merchants advertised specials and promoted their city as the home of the world's master carver.

Then, Sunday, June 16, was the big day. It ushered in the climax of Mooney Warther Week, complete with an antiques parade that included twenty cars, a steam engine, horse-

drawn carriages, a pony hitch and a circus calliope, plus a
queen, Mrs. A. L. (Edna) Cattabiani. The queen, to reflect the
fifty-year theme, had to be at least fifty years old!

At the end of the parade, in a Cadillac convertible covered
with gold foil, sat Mooney and Frieda. "When you boys do
something, you do it right," Frieda had told Bruce Mears
when he had picked her up in the shiny Cadillac prior to the
parade. She and Mooney had use of the automobile for the
entire week, but of course Mooney didn't dare sit behind the
wheel.

The parade rolled through the center of town, where it was
watched by seven thousand persons, and then out to Crater
Stadium, near the city's eastern boundary. There, two
thousand spectators appeared for the final ceremony of
Mooney Warther Week. Under the speaker's platform, which
had been set on the fifty yard line, was the draped bronze
bust that would soon be presented to the honored guest. The
Jaycees worried the presentation of the bust might be too
much of a shock for Mooney, who was now seventy-eight
years old, and so they advised him to be prepared for "an
unusual gift."

Following several short speeches, including one presented
by Mooney's friend, the Rev. Mr. Reinhard Krause, the
Jaycees' surprise was carried to the platform, set before
Mooney who was now standing, and uncovered. When
Mooney saw it, he squinted in the sunlight to focus his bleary
eyes on his remarkable image. His knees trembled and his
hand reached for the podium to catch himself. For the second
time in his life, the first being April 7, 1947, Mooney Warther
was speechless. He stood silently, his wife just behind him,
and gazed at the applauding audience. It was more of a gift
than he had ever imagined.

Later, Mooney reaffirmed his feelings of 1947 when he
said the bust and the celebration were the highest honors to
be bestowed upon any man.

The excitement of a new museum coupled with a week-long celebration charged Mooney's enthusiasm and he was eager to add several models to the Epics of Railroad History. To entertain his visitors during the special week, Mooney had started carving the Best Friend on June 10. The engine, from Charleston, South Carolina, had made history when it exploded and killed its inventor and a passenger. Mooney completed the model on September 12 and the following month, on his birthday, he began the Mississippi, the longest running steam engine in history. The locomotive had been built in the mid-1800s and during the Civil War it derailed and sank in a mud bank. Eleven years later the Mississippi was uncovered and it continued in operation through the 1920s. Mooney completed the Mississippi on Christmas Eve, 1963, and on Christmas he began carving the John Bull, one of America's first passenger trains, built in England in 1831. The John Bull was completed on Easter, 1964.

Mooney's momentum continued. Again, he was leading into a challenging task. On April 14, 1964, the ninety-ninth anniversary of the assassination of Abraham Lincoln, he began carving the entire funeral train of America's sixteenth president. Mooney, appropriately, used ebony and ivory to cut the engine, tender and three coaches, including the private train car that had been given to Lincoln at his second inaugural. The car, ironically, was a gift from the Southern Pacific Railroad which Lincoln had never used because it was bullet-proof and he felt it would have been cowardly to ride behind armor. The president's body lay in state in the car, however, and was transported west to Illinois for his funeral. Enroute, more than two million persons viewed Lincoln's body in its open casket, as the train stopped in various cities between the nation's capital and Springfield.

Mooney had always talked about carving the Funeral

Train of Abraham Lincoln, and he completed it on April 14, 1965, one year after he had cut the first slice in the model. The train culminated the carver's interest in the Great Emancipator and, now that he was nearly eighty years old, it was Mooney's final complex carving. A few months before he completed the model, Mooney received the Ohio Governor's Award, the state's most prestigious honor.

Old Ironsides, Mathias Baldwin's first engine built in 1832, followed the Funeral Train of Abraham Lincoln and it was completed on May 11, 1966. Mooney had begun the model on January 1 that year. Then, on September 3, 1966, Mooney began the Lady Baltimore, the most graceful of all locomotives, according to the carver, and the only engine that he carved to have chugged along the tracks below his home and the Calico Ditch. The Lady Baltimore would never be completed. The carving went slowly, painfully slowly. Mooney knew — in fact he said — he would leave the model unfinished. He wanted to leave the Lady Baltimore on his workbench. "Everyone should do something creative, and do it as long as you can until you die," Mooney claimed. "There's no hurry to finish it, no qualm about leaving it undone."

Chapter Twelve

The Final Years

During the summer months of the early 1960s, the daring swing in Mooney Warther's back yard drew an almost daily crowd of youngsters including Kenny Prince, Jimmy Eiler, Susan Fondriest, Michael Weigand, Larry Soulsby, John Warner, Kathy Kennedy and Kitty Warther, Mooney's niece. They were among the last generation of youngsters to know the great carver and the last to experience the thrill of a swing ride in his back yard. By the mid-1950s, Mooney's swing had become a famous landmark in Tuscarawas County and there was rarely a youngster in Dover who couldn't boast about his ride on the Great Elm. On a Sunday afternoon, children came from miles around just to wait in line for a ride over the Calico Ditch. Parents watched in fear, for the most part, if they looked at all. Occasionally, a dauntless adult waited a turn among the children in line. Mooney comforted the anxieties of his riders as he coaxed them onto the top platform from which they could experience the breathtaking ninety foot arc of the swing. "Take a ride to heaven," Mooney would tease as he helped a youngster onto the wooden seat of the swing and showed him how to grab hold of the thick cable that reached skyward and disappeared into the tree's limbs. Then the youngster was on his own — "Lift your feet and hold on," Mooney would advise — and the ride was beyond comparison. Not even the thrill of a roller coaster could match the shivering excitement of the swing on the Great Elm. One ride was not enough for most youngsters who mustered the courage for their first plunge, and as a result, the waiting line was never ending.

It was a sad day in 1968 when the swing had to be dismantled and the Great Elm chopped down. Dutch blight had destroyed the tree. Martha Hollinger, Frieda's sister, was there to take the final ride and watch the big tree fall. During its fifty year existence, the Great Elm had delighted the hearts of thousands of children, and without it, the Calico Ditch would soon be forgotten.

The end of the Great Elm marked the beginning of the demise of Mooney Warther. For all of his adult life, the tree swing had been Mooney's link to youth and now that the tree was gone, Mooney's age was youthless. He was eighty-three years old and failing. Time was now his most constant companion. The days of Mooney's final years were spent in the lobby of his museum. There he sat in front of his bronze bust which highlighted his Wall of Fame, covered with letters of praise from men like President Franklin D. Roosevelt, President Dwight D. Eisenhower, Vice-President Richard M. Nixon and General Omar Bradley. Mooney watched the faces of the youngsters and adults who came to see his Evolution of the Steam Engine. Occasionally, when he was able to whittle pliers, he'd gather a crowd around him, repeat his ageless stories in his hardy voice, and hand the pliers to spellbound youngsters. Children made old age difficult for Mooney. Not physically, but mentally. He saw in them the spirit of life and he envied their being. "Think that you can and do," he'd tell the children. "Never think anyone is trying to stop you or hinder you. Think that you can and do." Mooney thought his words, when heeded, were more valuable than even his carvings.

Physically, old age made Mooney's final years difficult. First, he suffered a stroke. Then, in July, 1971, he tripped and tumbled down two dozen concrete steps that led from his museum to his basement workshop. With two severe head lacerations and bruises to his shopworn body, Mooney was rushed to Union Hospital. Within several days his condition was "fair" and he was entertaining nurses and doctors and cheering up fellow patients, but Mooney's fall had been more damaging than anyone realized. Following a second stroke, he had fewer good days than bad days and Mooney could never return to 331 Karl Avenue. By the winter of 1971, Mooney had been moved to the hospital's extended care facility and then in April, 1972, he was transferred to the Dover Nursing Center, just a short walk from his home.

Frieda, who was now in her eighties, along with sons David and Tom and various other family members, saw Mooney every day, including days when he didn't know them. On the good days, Mooney entertained them, and when his old cronies — Hiner Richard, Don Frary, Herm Rieker, Chuck Mathias, Walter Richard — came to visit, he put on a show. "They're my medicine," he'd thunder at the nurse when she interrupted the visitors to give Mooney a dose of medication. "They'll do more good for me than anything in your bottles." Laughter had always been Mooney's medicine.

Another of Mooney's frequent visitors was the Rev. Mr. Reinhard Krause, then pastor of St. John's United Church of Christ. Other clergymen had wanted to visit Mooney, but he only had time for Reverend Krause, whom he admired for nearly thirty years.

"Oh yes, my old friend Krause," Mooney would whisper from his bed when the pastor came to visit near the end. "How is my friend Krause?"

Reverend Krause had more in common with Mooney than most men. He had grown up in Illinois and he, too, was a student of Lincoln. Consequently, the two men discussed Lincoln until Mooney's final day. "The country needs more men like Lincoln, Krause. Right now we need more men like

Lincoln," Mooney would repeat as he pointed to the photograph of Lincoln above his head. "Even at the end he's with me."

The minister knew that Mooney would not profit from a litany of comforting prayers, and so he offered none. Mooney could quote the Bible extensively, and Krause knew it. Moreover, he knew that Mooney Warther had prepared himself for death; he had granted death the same sound thinking that he had given life. Krause would save his prayers for Mooney's eulogy.

On June 8, 1973, Mooney Warther was dead. Death came ten years to the day after the carver had opened his modern museum. A six-column headline in the Times-Reporter, the city newspaper, announced the news and carried a lengthy obituary which began:

> The hands which carved a history of the evolution of steam and particularly the American railroad are still today.
>
> Death came quietly this morning to Ernest (Mooney) Warther as he lay in a coma in Dover Nursing Center. Infirmities brought on by age hospitalized Mooney two years ago and the last of a series of strokes Wednesday night was too much for the old man's heart.
>
> He was 87.

Because of Mooney's lingering illness, Frieda and her family were prepared for Mooney's death. Actually, in Frieda's eyes, the Boss had been gone for two years. And, after his fall, Karl Avenue did not expect to hear the noise of Mooney Warther again. Nonetheless, Mooney's death was felt. For most of eighty-seven years, and all but three of them active years, Mooney Warther had been Dover's personality and fame. He would be missed.

News of the death of the world's master carver traveled far as evidenced by the countless cards and letters of sympathy that were delivered to the most famous address on Dumb Street. Henry Morgan wrote from Canada that he had heard; that he had cried; and that he was sorry. From Michigan, Charlie Going, the promoter, wrote that long before he and Mooney had made a pact ". . . if I died before he died, he would not have to come to my funeral and cry, and if he died before I died, I would not have to go to his funeral and cry. And so my memory is of a wonderful, talented, exuberant and considerate man who was indeed the richest man in the world."

In Dover, Mooney's family and friends reflected on his life and times. His sister-in-law, Martha Hollinger, said she was one of the few people in Dover who understood Mooney Warther. "He was outspoken and so far ahead of everyone else that some people thought he was crazy. I understood him — he was a wonderful man who was good to kids, who didn't want to make a fuss, who loved peace and a good time."

Tom Moore, Jr., remembered, "I used to call him a dumb Swiss, but I thought he was a genius. He didn't like school and any man that never went to school past the second grade and made himself the smartest man that ever lived, was a genius."

Plenty of other people agreed with Tom Moore's summary of Mooney. Hiner Richard said his "freak mechanic and artistic abilities made him a genius." Walter Richard said, "No man living could do *one* of his trains in a lifetime let alone his entire collection."

The most poignant observation, perhaps, was offered by Mooney's oldest daughter, Florence, who said, "Pop, while being a very different man, was quite a man. Above all, he was a gentleman."

Some of Mooney's friends considered his talent a message

from God. "The Almighty wanted to show us what man could do with a penknife," said Vic Kuhn, the Big Engineer, "and He picked out Mooney Warther to show us." Helen Lahmers, who had played at Mooney's as a little girl, remarked, "God made Mooney special — his voice and hair — he was special and what he was doing was special. God wanted Mooney Warther to be outstanding."

In his rectory, the Rev. Mr. Krause was also reflecting about God and Mooney Warther. The pastor knew well in advance that he'd eventually have to write a memorial service for Mooney Warther, but now he found it the most challenging task of his ministry. While Mr. Krause had not always agreed with Mooney's thoughts on religion, he had found that in principle he quite often agreed with Mooney. "God, to Mooney, was not a supernatural being from whom we are separated," Krause said as he prepared to write Mooney's eulogy. "God, to Mooney, was an all-powerful and permeating force, not limited by space or time. And, most importantly, God was One with whom man was to work instructively." Krause underscored his thoughts and would stress them in his eulogy for Mooney Warther.

On the day of the funeral from St. John's, Reverend Krause preceded his prayer for Ernest Warther with this passage from John 8:32. *"And ye shall know the truth and the truth shall make you free."* Mooney had carved the verse on a walnut postcard and mailed it to his friend Krause in 1949.

Following the prayer, an obituary was read and a most thoughtful, penetrating eulogy. "Ernest Warther's spirit of industry and determination has been a source of inspiration for many. His achievements as a Master Carver have prompted acclaim and admiration from thousands in all walks and areas of life throughout our entire land and even in Mexico. And the community of Dover has qualified for lasting recognition and prominence because it has been the home of the Warthers," the pastor spoke before Mooney's mourners.

He analyzed and evaluated Mooney's efforts and endeavors. ". . . he was guided by a number of strong convictions. Among them his conviction that an all-powerful and an all-permeating force sustains and controls our entire universe. This prompted him to have the spirit of genuine gratitude in his heart and mind for the natural world with all of its wonders and beauties and unfailing certainties. An equally strong conviction which guided his efforts and endeavors was the conviction that human life is precious and that the privilege of living is every human being's greatest possession and that every life can be made to count in behalf of the well-being of others . . ."

The pastor closed Mooney's eulogy with this: ". . . death claimed him early Friday morning, June 8, 1973, when his life's course had attained to eighty-seven years, seven months and nine days. Those who survive him are the following: his devoted life's partner, Mrs. Frieda Warther; two sons, David and Thomas of Dover; three daughters, Florence, Mrs. Anker Jensen of Illinois; Alice, Mrs. Thomas McGuire of California; and Wilma, Mrs. Kenneth Ash of Colorado. A brother and a sister, Fred Warther and Mrs. Anna Meese of Dover. Surviving also are twenty-three grandchildren and nine great-grandchildren."

Of course, Mooney Warther was survived by more than family. He was survived by two generations of neighborhood gangs who cherished the events of life that he had etched in their minds. And he was survived by a museum in which he had captured the essence of the American steam locomotive. Mooney Warther was dead; but his immortality was guaranteed.

Book Notes

MOONEY, The Life of the World's Master Carver, has been written primarily from more than fifty interviews conducted by the author in the summer of 1975. Another primary source was Mooney Warther's diaries. These materials, for the most part, have not been available to the public. But with the release of this biography, the author's interviews have been consigned to the Warther Museum, Dover, Ohio, where they are available to students, researchers and scholars.

One point that requires clarification is Mooney's use of the title "the world's master carver." Various accounts have explained the title through the years. One report is that Henry Ford bestowed the epithet on Mooney. Another is that the famous carvers of Oberammergau granted him the honor. Neither account is accurate. By 1926 Mooney had billed himself as the "master carver" but in 1933 it was confirmed and "world's" was added to the title when Mooney won a wood carving contest sponsored by a popular magazine.

In two instances I have quoted passages from *The Little Boy Who Found a Knife* (1951) by Caroline J. Pardee. These quotes are used with permission of the author.